AQA English Literature A:
The Struggle for Identity
in Modern Literature

AS

Exclusively endorsed by AQA

Carol Leach

Nelson Thornes

Published in 2008 by:
Nelson Thornes Ltd
Delta Place
27 Bath Road
CHELTENHAM
GL53 7TH
United Kingdom

08 09 10 11 12 / 10 9 8 7 6 5 4 3 2

A catalogue record for this book is available from the British Library

ISBN 978 0 7487 8292 5

Cover photographs by Photolibrary and Alamy

Page make-up by Pantek Arts Ltd, Maidstone, Kent

Printed and bound in Croatia by Zrinski

Acknowledgements
Every effort has been made to contact copyright holders and we apologise if any have been inadvertently overlooked. The publisher will be happy to make any necessary amendments at reprint.

The authors and publisher would like to thank the following for permission to reproduce photographs and other copyright material:

p.9 © Mitchell Gerber/CORBIS; p.10 © Colin McPherson/Corbis; p.11 © Colin McPherson/Corbis; p.33 © Horst Tappe/Lebrecht Music & Ar; p.34 © Alastair Muir/Rex Features; p.36 © NILS JORGENSEN/Rex Features; p.44 © OKSANEN TESSA/CORBIS SYGMA; p.46 © 2005 Israel Police, Getty Images; p.48 © Sipa Press/Rex Features; p.51 © ARISTIDIS AFEIADAKIS/Alamy; p.54 © Gavriel Jecan/CORBIS; p.60 © Canham Portus Photos/Alamy; p.71 © Everett Collection/Rex Features; p.77 © 2007 Getty Images; p.81 © Alastair Muir/Rex Features; p.85 Nigel R. Barklie/Rex Features; p.88 Alastair Muir/ Rex Features; p.91 © c.HBO/Everett/Rex Features; p.94 © RORY MOORE/Alamy; p.97 © Getty Images; p.98 © AFP/Getty Images; p.99 © SUTTON-HIBBERT/Rex Features; p.100 © Bettmann/CORBIS.

Contents

AQA introduction

Nelson Thornes and AQA

Nelson Thornes has worked in collaboration with AQA to ensure that this book offers you the best support for your AS or A Level course and helps you to prepare for your exams. The partnership means that you can be confident that the range of learning, teaching and assessment practice materials has been checked by the senior examining team at AQA before formal approval, and is closely matched to the requirements of your specification.

Blended learning

Printed and electronic resources are blended: this means that links between topics and activities between the book and the electronic resources help you to work in the way that best suits you, and enable extra support to be provided online. For example, you can test yourself online and feedback from the test will direct you back to the relevant parts of the book.

Electronic resources are available in a simple-to-use online platform called Nelson Thornes learning space. If your school or college has a licence to use the service, you will be given a password through which you can access the materials through any internet connection.

Icons in this book indicate where there is material online related to that topic. The following icons are used:

Learning activity

These resources include a variety of interactive and non-interactive activities to support your learning.

Progress tracking

These resources include a variety of tests that you can use to check your knowledge on particular topics (Test yourself) and a range of resources that enable you to analyse and understand examination questions (On your marks…).

Research support

These resources include WebQuests, in which you are assigned a task and provided with a range of web links to use as source material for research.

Study skills

These resources support you as you develop a skill that is key for your course, for example planning essays.

Analysis tool

These resources help you to analyse key texts and images by providing questions and prompts to focus your response.

When you see an icon, go to Nelson Thornes learning space at **www.nelsonthornes.com/aqagce**, enter your access details and select your course. The materials are arranged in the same order as the topics in the book, so you can easily find the resources you need.

How to use this book

This book covers the specification for your course and is arranged in a sequence approved by AQA. The book is divided into eight chapters, beginning, in Chapter 1 with an introduction to the English Literature A Specification and how you will be assessed. Chapters 2 and 3 explain your exam and coursework tasks and texts. Chapters 4 to 6 each provide guidance on your wider reading in the genres of poetry, prose and drama. Chapter 7 helps to familiarise you with the context question, exploring examples of the type of extracts you might be expected to deal with in the examination. Finally, Chapter 8 takes you through an examination paper, demonstrating how to tackle the paper and focus your answer using keywords.

Aims of the chapter

At the beginning of each section you will find a list of learning objectives that contain targets linked to the requirements of the specification.

The features in this book include:

Key terms

Terms that you will need to be able to define and understand. These terms are coloured blue in the textbook and their definition will also appear in the glossary at the back of this book.

Did you know?

Interesting facts to extend your background knowledge.

Links

Links to refer you to other areas of the book which cover the topics you are reading about.

Further reading

Suggestions for other texts that will help you in your study and preparation for assessment in English literature.

Activity

Activities which develop the skills you will need for success in your English literature course.

Questions

Questions which help to focus your reading of key extracts and prepare you for writing on extracts in the exam and in your coursework.

AQA Examination-style questions

Questions in the style that you can expect in your exam. You will find these in Chapter 8.

Summary

A summary of what is covered in each chapter of the book.

AQA examination questions are reproduced by permission of the Assessment and Qualifications Alliance.

1 Introduction

Aims of the chapter:

- Introduces the content and skills of the AS course.

- Considers the philosophy of reading and meaning that underpins the Specification.

- Explores the choices you can make in your wider reading.

- Explains how you will be assessed.

This book has been written to help you to be as successful as possible in your AS AQA English Literature A course. It will introduce you to the relevant **subject matter** that you need to **know and understand**, as well as to the **skills** you need to develop and apply in order to read, analyse, interpret and write about your texts.

In this chapter we look at:

- the kinds of reading you will be undertaking
- the wider reading list
- the Assessment Objectives
- the marking grid.

This book will give you help, support and advice on:

- how to approach your set texts
- how to succeed with your coursework
- how to tackle wider reading in prose, poetry and drama
- approaches to wider reading in non-fiction
- a sample exam paper.

Your AS English Literature course

This is one of three AS textbooks for AQA English Literature A, one each for the three optional areas of study. Your chosen option is 'The Struggle for Identity in Modern Literature', which is the focus for this book and all your reading for the AS course. You will be studying **one poetry** text for the written exam, and **one prose** text and **one drama** text for your coursework.

You will also need to read widely in modern literature which embodies a struggle for identity. Your wider reading will probably include some whole texts, but will no doubt also include a good many extracts. Reading the extracts will help you to appreciate the variety and range of modern literature about struggles for identity, covering writers of both **genders**, as well as texts of all **genres**.

Your teacher will establish the foundation and framework for your reading, but as you progress through your AS course, and once you gain confidence and experience as a reader, **you** should increasingly be the one who chooses and explores aspects of the literature. You will then be in a position to be able to pursue your own interests, tracing connections, comparisons and contrasts between texts in the **shared context** of modern literature about a struggle for identity. Your study of the chosen area of literature will therefore consist of both **close and wide reading**.

How to become an informed, independent reader

Before we start to explore your chosen area of literature, we are going to establish what kind of reader you need to be. The aim of AS English Literature is to enable you to develop as an informed, independent reader and confident critic of literary texts.

As an informed, independent reader, you will learn to build a reading of a text through:

■ careful and close reading which provides you with appropriate and specific evidence to support your interpretation

■ consideration and understanding of other possible readings

■ research into the contexts of both reading and writing.

The AQA English Literature A Specification provides you, the reader, with maximum opportunities for both writing coursework and for sitting an open-text exam (an exam where you are allowed to take a copy of your set text into the exam and are encouraged to use it to help answer the questions). Such opportunities encourage research on the one hand and close focus on specific parts of texts on the other.

Reading for meaning

As you read the literature of your chosen period, you will need to be **actively engaged** with your texts in order to develop **informed, personal responses**.

The AQA English literature course is built on a philosophy of reading and meaning which it is important that you understand and share.

We think that:

Reading:

■ is an active process: the reader is an **active creator**, not a passive recipient of second-hand opinion – *you are the 'maker of meaning'*

■ can never be 'innocent': all readings are historically, socially and individually specific – *you bring your own personal context and experience to the text*

■ is not a single skill: some kinds of reading are more demanding than others – *think, for example, of the comparable difficulty of reading a Mills and Boon romance on the one hand, and a Jane Austen novel on the other.*

Meaning:

■ for an individual reader, depends as much on what is brought to the text as on what is contained within it – *your own experience will influence the way you read the text*

■ will not necessarily be instantly accessible – *you may well need to research difficult or obscure references and vocabulary, for example, before you can tease out meaning*

■ will be different on different occasions, and changeable as a result of discussion and reflection – *when you reread a text, for example, you may find your response is different from your first reading; discussion with your peers and/or your teacher or reading a critical commentary may also influence and change your response to a text*

■ can be multiple; different readings of a text can coexist – *you need to be aware that some texts are ambiguous or capable of delivering multiple meanings, and it is your own selection of and response to textual evidence that will determine your own personal interpretation.*

Wider reading for your AS English Literature A course

Your AS course, then, is a coherent collection of reading in modern literature about different struggles for identity. The texts for detailed study (the set poetry text in the exam and the novel and play in your coursework) are supported by your wider reading, which provides the context.

The purpose of your wider reading is to:

■ provide you with the opportunity to discover and explore your own interests and enjoyment, developing your awareness of the ways you respond to and understand different kinds of writing

■ enable you to consider the **typicality** or **shared context** of your reading so that you can explore connections, comparisons and contrasts

■ encourage you to see different points of view, exploring the ways that different writers describe a similar experience or situation

■ enable you to discover and understand the ways different writers choose to communicate with you, the reader, exploring choices of form, structure and language.

The Specification for the AQA AS English Literature A course provides you with a reading list from which you and your teachers can choose whole texts and extracts for study. It covers all relevant **genres**, writing by both **male and female** authors, significant and influential **literature in translation,** as well as **non-fiction** texts. The wider reading list is set out below.

Texts for AS – The Struggle for Identity in Modern Literature

* denotes text published after 1990

+ denotes text published between 1800 and 1945

Note also that the date at the end of the text is the earliest known published date. The publisher details are for currently available editions.

Wider reading in Unit 1

Choose three texts (or the equivalent in extracts) of any genre.

Prose fiction
Any of the 10 named texts for Unit 2 or any other novel by Toni Morrison, plus:

Chinua Achebe, *Things Fall Apart* (Penguin, 1958)

James Baldwin, *Go Tell It on the Mountain* (Penguin, 1954)

Nadine Gordimer, *July's People* (Bloomsbury, 1981)

+Radclyffe Hall, *The Well of Loneliness* (Virago, 1928)

+Zora Neale Hurston, *Their Eyes Were Watching God* (Virago, 1937)

*Andrea Levy, *Small Island* (Headline, 2004)

*Patrick McCabe, *Breakfast on Pluto* (Picador, 1998)

*Anne Michaels, *Fugitive Pieces* (Bloomsbury, 1996)

*Arundhati Roy, *The God of Small Things* (Harper Perennial, 1997)

+Robert Tressell, *The Ragged-Trousered Philanthropists* (Flamingo, 1914)

Kurt Vonnegut, *Slaughterhouse 5* (Vintage, 1969)

*Irvine Welsh, *Trainspotting* (Vintage, 1993)

Jeanette Winterson, *Oranges Are Not the Only Fruit* (Vintage, 1984)

+Richard Wright, *Native Son* (Vintage, 1940)

Prose non-fiction
Autobiography, biography and diaries

Maya Angelou, *Autobiography*, especially *I Know Why the Caged Bird Sings* (Virago, 1969)

*Diana Souhami, *The Trials of Radclyffe Hall* (Virago, 1999)

Memoirs and interviews

*Silvia Calamati, *Women's Stories from the North of Ireland* (Beyond the Pale Publications, 2002)

Bobby Sands, *Skylark Sing Your Lonely Song* (Mercier Press, 1982)

*Alice Walker, *The Same River Twice: Honoring the Difficult* (Phoenix, 1996)

Malcolm X, *Malcolm X Talks to Young People* (Pathfinder, 1964–5)

Travelogues

Salman Rushdie, *The Jaguar Smile: A Nicaraguan Journey* (Vintage, 1987)

History and cultural commentary, essays and speeches

David Beresford, *Ten Men Dead: The Story of the 1981 Hunger Strike* (Harper Collins, 1987)

Beverly Bryan, Suzanne Scafe and Stella Dadzie, *The Heart of the Race* (Virago, 1985)

Germaine Greer, *The Female Eunuch* (Harper Perennial, 1970)

Martin Luther King Jr, *I Have a Dream: Writings and Speeches That Changed the World* (Harper, 1956–68)

*Adhaf Soueif, *Mezzaterr – Fragments from the Common Ground* (Bloomsbury, 2004)

Amrit Wilson, *Dreams, Questions, Struggles: South Asian Women in Britain* (Pluto Press, 2006)

Laws

Parliament 'Section 28 of the Education Act' (1988)

Literary criticism

Ralph Ellison, *Shadow and Act* (Vintage, 1967)

Jeremy Hawthorn ed., *The British Working Class Novel in the Twentieth Century* (Hodder Arnold, 1984)

*Dolly A. McPherson, *Order out of Chaos: The Autobiographical Works of Maya Angelou* (Virago, 1990)

Kate Millet, *Sexual Politics* (Virago, 1977)

Amrit Wilson, *Finding a Voice: Asian Women in Britain* (Virago, 1978)

+Richard Wright, *Blueprint for Negro Writing* (1937)

Drama

Samuel Beckett, *Endgame* (Faaber, 1958)

Brendan Behan, *The Hostage* (Methuen, 1958)

*Sudha Bhuchar, *Child of the Divide* (Methuen Modern Plays, 2006)

Jim Cartwright, *Road* (Methuen Modern Plays, 1986)

*Caryl Churchill – all plays (some will be post-1990)

*Claire Dowie, *Why is John Lennon Wearing a Skirt?* (Methuen Modern Plays, 1996)

*Brian Friel, *Dancing at Lughnasa* (Faber, 1990)

Lorraine Hansberry, *A Raisin in the Sun* (Methuen Modern Plays, 1959)

*Tony Kushner, *Angels in America* (Nick Herne Books, 1992)

*Martin Macdonagh, *Beauty Queen of Leenane* (Methuen, 1996)

Arthur Miller, *Death of a Salesman* (Penguin, 1949)

+Sean O'Casey, *Three Dublin Plays: Juno and the Paycock* (1924), *The Plough and the Stars* (1926), *Shadow of a Gunman* (1923) (Faber)

*Mark Ravenhill, *Citizenship* (Methuen Modern Plays, 2006)

*Ntozake Shange, *Shange Plays 1* (includes *For Colored Girls Who Have Considered Suicide* (Methuen, 2002)

Timberlake Wertenbaker, *Our Country's Good* (Methuen, 1988)

Tennessee Williams, *A Streetcar Named Desire* (Methuen, 1947)

*International Connections (contributor Jackie Kay), *New Plays for Young People* (Faber, 2003)

Poetry

*Simon Armitage, *Dead Sea Poems* (Faber, 1995)

+W.H. Auden (e.g. 'The Quarry', 'Refugee Blues', 'Funeral Blues') (1930s)

Gillian Clarke, *Letters from a Far Country* (1985)

*Carol Ann Duffy, *The Other Country* (Anvil, 1990)

Alan Ginsberg, *Howl* (City Lights Pocket Poet Series, 1956)

+Langston Hughes, *Collected Poems* (Vintage, 1930–60)

*Jackie Kay, *Life Mask* (Bloodaxe Books, 2005)

Liz Lochhead, *Dreaming Frankenstein and Collected Poems* (Polygon, 1984)

*Audre Lorde – any (some will be post-1990)

Grace Nichols, *The Fat Black Woman's Poems* (Virago, 1984)

*Adrienne Rich, *The School among the Ruins* (Norton, 2004)

*Lemn Sissay, *Morning Breaks in the Elevator* (Payback Press, 1999)

*Lemn Sissay (ed.), *The Fire People: A Collection of Contemporary Black British Poets* (Payback Press, 1998)

+Gertrude Stein, *Tender Buttons* (Dover, 1914)

Alice Walker, *Revolutionary Petunias and Other Poems* (Harcourt Brace Jovanovitch, 1970)

*Benjamin Zephaniah, *Too Black, Too Strong* (Bloodaxe Books, 2001)

Texts in translation

Novels

Isabel Allende, *The House of the Spirits* (Chile/Spanish) (Black Swan, 1985)

+Alexandra Kollontai, *Love of Worker Bees* (USSR/Russian) (Virago, 1930)

Manuel Puig, *Kiss of the Spider Woman* (Argentina/ Spanish) (Vintage, 1976)

Alexander Solzhenitsyn, *One Day in the Life of Ivan Denisovitch* (USSR/Russian) (Penguin, 1962)

Poetry

+Pablo Neruda, *Residence on Earth* (Chile/Spanish) (Souvenir Press, 1933)

Drama

+Bertolt Brecht, *Mother Courage and her Children* (German) (Methuen, 1940)

+Federico García Lorca, *The House of Bernada Alba* (1936), *Yerma* (1934), *Blood Wedding* (1933) (Spanish) (Penguin)

Non-fiction: autobiography/diary/travelogue

Anne Frank, *The Diary of a Young Girl* (Dutch) (Penguin, 1947)

Che Guevara, *The Motorcycle Diaries* (Argentina/ Spanish) (Harper Perennial, 1952)

Nawal al-Saadawi, *Memoirs from the Women's Prison* (Egypt/Arabic) (1984)

Keeping a record of your reading will be very important, especially as you will be dealing with a good many extracts. We suggest that you keep a detailed **Reading Log**; at the end of the course this will provide a valuable revision tool. Another useful thing to do would be to place all your reading in the shared context on a **timeline**.

Close reading for your AS English Literature course

Not only is it important that you read widely throughout the course, but you must also ensure that you develop the skills of **close reading**. You will need these skills in every answer you write and they underpin the whole of your AS English Literature course.

Close reading of a text will enable you to **analyse** and **explore** a writer's techniques – his or her choices of form, structure and language – and will also help you to:

- respond fully to meaning or possible meanings of the text
- gain understanding of the ways texts work
- find textual evidence to support your interpretation.

If you are the kind of reader who does **not** read closely, you will only be able to offer a **skimpy** reading of your texts, based on **unsupported assertion**. This will not be sufficient for you to be successful in your AS English Literature course. Neither is there any point in counting numbers of syllables, making exaggerated claims for alliteration, or setting out a pattern of rhyme (ababcc, for example), unless this research is part of an analysis or exploration of the ways the writer's choices make meaning for you.

It is important that you adopt good reading habits:

- You should read every whole text or extract three or four times in order to mine it thoroughly; the first reading will be for general impression, the subsequent ones will enable you to explore the writer's techniques fully.
- Initially you will respond to subject matter and theme.
- Then you need to move on to the ways the writer expresses the subject matter.

In order to analyse the ways writers write, you need to ask yourself particular questions:

- What kind of text is this?
- When was this text written?
- What is the subject matter?

■ Who is speaking and how does the writer use the idea of 'voice' in the text?

■ How does the writer use setting(s)?

■ How does the writer use ideas of time? (past, present, future)

■ How does the writer structure, organise and develop the ideas in the text?

■ Is there anything distinctive in the way the text is written? (structure, choices of vocabulary, sentence structures, variations in pace ...)

■ Are there any patterns, repetitions of key ideas or images or uses of contrast?

■ What kinds of language are used? (formal, informal, descriptive, dialogue, and so on)

■ How has finding out more about the references and allusions in the text added to my understanding and interpretation?

■ Is the language all the same or does the writer use contrast?

■ What is the tone of the text?

■ What might be the writer's purpose in this text?

All the answers to these questions need to be related to your own interpretation of the text, and to your own making of meaning.

How your work will be assessed

Your wider reading in the poetry, prose and drama of 'The Struggle for Identity in Modern Literature', as well as your knowledge and understanding of your chosen poetry text, will be assessed in Unit 1. You will write two essays in a two-hour exam. This unit carries 60 per cent of AS or 30 per cent of A2 marks. In Unit 2 (coursework) you will write two more essays, one on your prose text and one on your drama text. The folder as a whole will be about 2,500 words in length and carries 40 per cent of AS or 20 per cent of A2 marks.

All your work for the course will be assessed against four Assessment Objectives (AOs):

AO1 Articulate creative, informed and relevant responses to literary texts, using appropriate terminology and concepts, and coherent, accurate written expression (*your ability to use your knowledge and understanding, to focus on the task, and to express yourself appropriately*).

AO2 Demonstrate detailed critical understanding in analysing the ways in which structure, form and language shape meanings in literary texts (*your ability to explore the ways the writers' choices of form, structure and language influence the ways you interpret texts and make meaning*).

AO3 Explore connections and comparisons between different literary texts, informed by interpretations of other readers (*your ability to find links between the texts you read and to explore alternative readings*).

AO4 Demonstrate understanding of the significance and influence of the contexts in which literary texts are written and received (*your ability to assess where and how your texts fit into the shared context*).

These four Assessment Objectives are used to measure your achievement throughout the Specification and are organised by your examiners into a marking grid which is used to assess each piece of work that you do throughout your course.

You, and your teachers, will be able to check your performance against the criteria in the grid. Each of the AOs is divided into 'bands' (see the table on page 7).

If your work has the features of **Band 1** work – inaccurate, irrelevant, assertive – you will not be writing at the required standard for AS.

If your work is assessed as falling into **Band 2**, it is judged to be narrative and descriptive and rather generalised in its approach to text.

If your work is assessed as falling within **Band 3**, then it means that you are starting to explore and analyse the texts and presenting your work in a coherent fashion.

If your work is assessed as falling into **Band 4,** it is coherent, cogent, mature and sophisticated, and worthy of the highest grade.

Marking grid for Units 1 and 2

	Assessment Objectives			
	AO1	**AO2**	**AO3**	**AO4**
	AO1: Articulate creative, informed and relevant responses to literary texts, using appropriate terminology and concepts, and coherent, accurate written expression	AO2: Demonstrate detailed critical understanding in analysing the ways in which structure, form and language shape meanings in literary texts	AO3: Explore connections and comparisons between different literary texts, informed by interpretations of other readers	AO4: Demonstrate understanding of the significance and influence of the contexts in which literary texts are written and received
Band 1	Candidates characteristically: ■ communicate limited knowledge and understanding of literary texts ■ make few uses of appropriate terminology or examples to support interpretations ■ attempt to communicate meaning by using inaccurate language.	Candidates characteristically: ■ identify few aspects of structure, form and language ■ assert some aspects with reference to how they shape meaning.	Candidates characteristically: ■ make few links between literary texts ■ reflect the views expressed in other interpretations of literary texts in a limited way.	Candidates characteristically: ■ communicate limited understanding of context through descriptions of culture, text type, literary genre or historical period.
Band 2	Candidates characteristically: ■ communicate some basic knowledge and understanding of literary texts ■ make simple use of appropriate terminology or examples to support interpretations ■ communicate meaning using straightforward language.	Candidates characteristically: ■ identify obvious aspects of structure, form and language ■ describe some aspects with reference to how they shape meaning.	Candidates characteristically: ■ make straightforward links and connections between literary texts ■ reflect the views expressed in other interpretations of literary texts in a basic way.	Candidates characteristically: ■ communicate some basic understanding of context through descriptions of culture, text type, literary genre or historical period.
Band 3	Candidates characteristically: ■ communicate relevant knowledge and understanding of literary texts ■ present relevant responses, using appropriate terminology to support informed interpretations ■ structure and organise their writing ■ communicate content and meaning through expressive and accurate writing.	Candidates characteristically: ■ identify relevant aspects of structure, form and language in literary texts ■ explore how writers use specific aspects to shape meaning ■ use specific references to texts to support their responses.	Candidates characteristically: ■ explore links and connections between literary texts ■ communicate understanding of the views expressed in different interpretations or readings.	Candidates characteristically: ■ communicate understanding of the relationships between literary texts and their contexts ■ comment appropriately on the influence of culture, text type, literary genre or historical period on the ways in which literary texts were written and were – and are – received.

	Candidates characteristically:	Candidates characteristically:	Candidates characteristically:	Candidates characteristically:
Band 4	■ communicate relevant knowledge and understanding of literary texts with confidence ■ present relevant, well-informed responses, fluently using appropriate terminology to support informed interpretations ■ structure and organise their writing in a cogent manner ■ communicate content and meaning through sophisticated and mature writing.	■ identify relevant aspects of structure, form and language in literary texts ■ confidently explore how writers use specific aspects to shape meaning ■ show a mastery of detail in their use of specific texts to support their responses.	■ explore links and connections between literary texts with confidence ■ communicate understanding of the views expressed in different interpretations or readings in a mature, sophisticated manner.	■ communicate a mature understanding of the relationships between literary texts and their contexts ■ comment in a sophisticated manner on the influence of culture, text type, literary genre or historical period on the ways in which literary texts were written and were – and are – received.

Summary

We have now considered:

■ the kind of reading you will be doing

■ the choices you will be making

■ the skills you need to develop

■ how your work will be assessed.

We now turn to an exploration of the detail of your studies. Each of the sections in this book looks at a different part of your AS English Literature course in more detail:

■ the set texts for Unit 1

■ coursework for Unit 2

■ wider reading in the three genres – poetry, prose and drama

■ how to prepare for the context question in your written exam

■ looking at a sample exam paper and how to get the best possible marks in your answer.

We begin in the next chapter with a consideration of the set poetry text on the written paper.

2 How to approach the set text in Unit 1

Aims of the chapter:

■ Introduces the set poetry text.

■ Suggests the best and most effective ways to approach the study of your set text in this unit.

■ Explains how you will be assessed in the exam.

Fig. 2.1 *Maya Angelou*

💡 Choice of text

There are three poetry texts set for study on this paper; you will study **one** of them. We look here at what each one offers in terms of the poetry that embodies 'The Struggle for Identity' and how each poet approaches this idea across their collection.

You will be studying one of the following texts.

Either

🗲 💡 1 *And Still I Rise* by Maya Angelou, published by Virago, 1986 (first published by Random House, 1978)

Some background

When *And Still I Rise* was first published, Angelou was already an established figure on the American black literary scene. This poetry collection was her third, published when she was 50 years old, around the time of the publication of the second and third volumes of her autobiography. The most famous, volume one, *I Know Why the Caged Bird Sings*, first published in 1969, is included in the non-fiction texts as part of your wider reading list.

💡 *The poetry*

The title *And Still I Rise* crystallises the concerns of this collection and captures perfectly her response to prejudice, to a lifetime of personal and political struggle, and to those who marginalise her still. In modern literature, this collection offers a poetic exploration of 'struggle' and an engagement with the world around her through, as Angelou herself once said, not merely 'surviving' but 'thriving' – and 'rising'.

The collection

The collection has 32 poems which Angelou has grouped into three sections:

Part One: Touch me, Life, Not Softly (8 poems)

Part Two: Traveling (15 poems)

Part Three: And Still I Rise (9 poems).

Each section offers a poetic 'struggle for identity' in different ways. The subject matter of *Part One: Touch me, Life, Not Softly* focuses on a personal awakening. The adult sense of self now established, *Part Two: Traveling* then considers a wider experience, and goes beyond exploration of the 'self' into social exploration. *Part Three: And Still I Rise* takes its name from the title of the whole collection. It is the poetic conclusion to the struggles of self and social identity and survival traced through the previous two sections. The keynote poem, 'Still I Rise', sets the tone here: optimistic and defiant. In this collection, *And Still I Rise*, the poet encourages the reader to consider how and if these struggles have been overcome. In this chapter, we ask you to engage with how this has been achieved poetically.

Or

🔲 🔲 2 *The World's Wife* by Carol Ann Duffy, published by Picador, 1999

Some background

Carol Ann Duffy has become something of a celebrity poet, achieving the 'rock-and-roll' fame long denied to Angelou's generation, early in her poetic career and publication history. Considered but rejected for Poet Laureate, the world was perhaps not quite ready for mainstreaming the feminist voice of collections like *The World's Wife*. Accepted in good spirit, this did not affect her swift rise to fame: consistently chosen poet for literary study at GCSE, A-level and university for the past generation of students; teacher and professor of creative writing MA courses; frequent speaker and reader at student conferences; interview subject in a national weekend newspaper supplement.

💡 The collection

In common with the Angelou collection, *The World's Wife* challenges the past and our view of its legacy.

Fig. 2.2 *Carol Ann Duffy*

The idea of seeing women **solely** as a 'wife' and therefore without a separate identity or sense of self, as an individual or as part of a social group, is rejected, along with the notion of male social dominance, 'the world' itself. This idea can be seen in the choice of subject matter not only to redress the historical imbalance, but also to 're-imagine' and redefine the present. The effect is perhaps a wider, more representative, more inclusive view of women and the roles and responsibilities they deserve.

We have in *The World's Wife* an exploration of fulfilled female identities that have gone beyond merely 'wife' to 'the world', at work and at home, yet it does not seem that Duffy glorifies or romanticises what it means to be female. In this collection women can be good or bad; the main point is that they can simply *be*, after struggling against the 'threatened' obstacles which have been put in their way, across considerable time and many cultures.

Or

🔲 💡 3 *Skirrid Hill* by Owen Sheers, published by Seren, 2005

Some background

Owen Sheers is another interesting character. Born on the idyllic Pacific island of Fiji and bred in the beautiful valleys of south Wales from where his family hail, his travels and work have led him to Zimbabwe, New York, Croatia, Hungary and now London. This international backdrop can be seen in the border-crossing feast of contrasts and variety which influence his choices of poetic form and subject matter.

Adept in all literary genres, since 2000 he has been acclaimed for his writing: for his poetry, first with *The Blue Book* in 2000; then with his non-fiction prose work in 2004, *The Dust Diaries*, set in Zimbabwe and exploring an intriguing family connection; followed in 2006 by a play, *Unicorns*, starring Joseph Fiennes at the Old Vic theatre in London; in 2007 for his first novel *Resistance*, in which he feels 'the Welsh landscape is the most important muse', where 'The Valleys influence the actions and mindset of those characters'.

💡 *The collection*

Skirrid Hill is a collection of 41 poems which in some ways deal with an attempt to be defined. To find your identity and carve a space where you cannot be forgotten or ignored – as a person, in a relationship, in a place, as part of a people, in time, in history – these concerns echo through the poetry in different forms. The text offers a note on the title, telling us that the name 'Skirrid' comes 'from the Welsh . . . Ysgariad meaning divorce or separation'. If you know the hill itself, 'standing broken-backed on the border, gazing east over England, west over Wales', as Sarah Crown eloquently summarised in a *Guardian* review of the collection, then you might wonder if we are being offered poems that deal with belonging and loss, and the bewilderment and desolation this can bring.

To summarise:

All three texts offer you a rich selection of poetry which explores many struggles for identity in modern literature, but there are key differences between them in terms of the **subject matter**, the **context or background** which affects its publication, and the poet's **approaches and purposes**:

Fig. 2.3 *Owen Sheers*

- Angelou focuses on the experiences of **black women and men** in her lifetime and for her American and African predecessors, ranging across forms to explore their **self and social identities**.
- Duffy focuses on the experiences of **women, in particular as wives**, and tries to present a world which foregrounds female perspectives **using famous historical and cultural characters and reference points** as a framework.
- Sheers focuses on **loss and separation**, and **uses place and setting**, often – but not exclusively – that of his homeland of Wales, to explore **fractured but deeply held identities**.

🔍 Studying the poems in your chosen text

Once you have chosen your poetry text, you will need to do all you can to make sure you are familiar with the whole anthology, and that you understand each poem.

You will need to study each poem individually, as well as the collection as a whole. Here are some suggestions for how you could go about doing this.

1 For each poem:
   - Look back to the section on close reading in Chapter 1 and use the prompts and questions to work with each poem.
   - Make a note of your responses to the questions, of the ways you interpret the poem, and of how it reflects experiences of a struggle for identity.
   - Start a **Reading Log** where you record your responses to each poem. This may be organised in a paper file, or by using the online Reading Log provided for you. You can save this and add to it throughout your course. You can also print it out for revision.

2 For the whole collection:
   - Go on to consider how the individual poems connect and compare with each other, in terms of subject matter and style.
   - Look at the way the poet has structured the text and explore why you think she or he chose to arrange it in this way.
   - Try arranging the poems in a different way and assess the changed impact the new structure has on the reader.

The notes you assemble from these activities will help you to produce very useful notes for your revision.

The Assessment Objectives for Unit 1

When you have read and studied your poems closely, you need to consider the ways in which you will prepare for the exam. Clearly your preparation needs to be informed by the way you will be assessed. We looked at the Assessment Objectives in some detail in Chapter 1, and you may wish to remind yourself of what they are and how they work.

For your set text, there are **three** relevant Assessment Objectives:

AO1 – *your ability to use your knowledge and understanding, to focus on the task, and to express yourself appropriately.*

AO2 – *your ability to explore the ways the writers' choices of form, structure and language influence the ways you interpret texts and make meaning.*

AO3 – *your ability to find links between the poems you study and to explore alternative readings.*

You will be assessed on your ability to meet all three Assessment Objectives, but you will need to remember that the **most important** Assessment Objective is **AO3** – your ability **to connect and compare the poems** as well as **to consider different interpretations.**

What kinds of questions will you have to answer in the exam?

The three relevant Assessment Objectives are reflected in every question set on your chosen poetry text. You will be given a choice of two questions, and you will answer one of them. All the questions test the same Assessment Objectives.

Each question will set out a view which you are invited to consider. You will need to say how far you agree with the view in the question.

A few examples of the kinds of views that may be expressed in the questions are:

- a named poem as the key to the collection
- a named poem as an appropriate introduction to the collection
- a named poem as an appropriate conclusion to the collection
- the collection has little variety
- the collection lacks coherence
- many of the poems in the collection have no literary merit.

You can make up your own questions using some or all of these suggestions, swap them with other students and attempt to answer each other's questions. This should help you to develop the receptive, open-minded approach to the ideas of others that is one of the keys to exam success.

Remember that you need to consider the view, saying how far you agree, through consideration and comparison of poems in the collection. Most questions invite you to consider two or three poems in some detail or to range more widely.

How will I be assessed in the exam?

Examiners will use the four-band marking grid which was introduced in Chapter 1. They will assess your essay out of 45, using a mark scheme tailored to each question; this will relate to:

- the three relevant Assessment Objectives
- the four-band marking grid
- the keywords of the question.

Summary

Advice for success:

- Remember that this is still an English literature exam. Although the questions on your set text will be testing Assessment Objective 3 in particular, meeting Assessment Objectives 1 and 2 is still vital to your success. You will need to be able to write clear, structured answers; you will also need to have a secure knowledge of the text and show that you are able to analyse the writer's use of language and style.

- You will meet the Assessment Objectives if you produce a relevant answer that addresses the keywords of the question you choose; the wording and construction of all the questions are designed to point you towards the appropriate Assessment Objectives.

- Look carefully at the Assessment Grids in Chapter 8: there is a detailed, generic version which applies to all questions, and a question-specific version for each of the questions on your set text. The examiners will be using these grids when they mark your set-text answer: the descriptors for each level and Assessment Objective will give you some idea of what they will be looking for.

- You should try to develop the skills necessary for the construction of a balanced argument: these are vital because you will meet Assessment Objective 3 by writing a relevant answer to the question 'How far do you agree?'

- You should try to think for yourself when responding to your chosen set-text question. Although it is not compulsory, you may refer to any critics you have read if you wish to. However, **your own ideas** are the most important: the question will invite you to express your answer in the first person.

- Remember that, as this is an open-book exam, there will usually be a question that requires you to focus on a specific poem or group of poems.

- It is important that you back up your ideas by close reference to the poetry when answering your set-text question, but keep the quotations short: examiners know that a candidate who copies out large chunks of the text is probably struggling to cope.

- Remember that you are expected to be familiar with the whole of the poetry selection you have studied.

- Make the effort to read around the **set text** you are studying. Wider reading can provide important background information on your set poet in the context of 'The Struggle for Identity in Modern Literature', as well as giving you the chance to consider other perspectives on the poetry which will help you to address Assessment Objective 3.

> **Link**
>
> If you turn to Chapter 8 you will see sample poetry questions on a specimen paper, as well as an outline of marking criteria.

What to avoid:

■ Do not respond to the exam question by writing an account of a poet's life and times. A successful answer to the question might include some relevant biographical information, but it is important that you display your contextual knowledge *through* your knowledge of the poetry. The bit of background you have been given on each poet is to show you who you are dealing with, arouse your curiosity about their work and whet your appetite for the poetry. It is not to provide you with some notes to give back to us in the exam, made irrelevant in the retelling – so don't!

■ Do not write an answer that wholly agrees (or disagrees) with the view that is set up for discussion in the question: such a one-sided, unbalanced response will be given a Band 2 mark, no matter how good your textual knowledge is, because you will not have met Assessment Objective 3.

■ Do not abuse the open-book exam by copying anything out of the introduction or the notes included in your set text: the examiners will spot what you have done, and they know that anyone who tries it must be desperate: unassimilated critical material is often a feature of Band 1 answers.

■ Do not recycle your practice answers when you sit the exam. The questions are never the same as those set previously, so twisting an earlier essay in an attempt to fit it to a new question usually ends in disaster. You must approach each question afresh.

3 Approaching the coursework

Introduction

For Unit 2 you will be asked to present a folder of coursework that contains **two** pieces of writing: one will be an essay on a **prose** text, the other on a **drama** text. Both texts will come from the **shared context** of 'The Struggle for Identity in Modern Literature'. You will be given a list of 10 prose texts and a list of 3 drama texts from which you make your choices. When you have studied your two chosen texts, you will then negotiate the two tasks with your teacher. Your teacher will make sure that both of your agreed tasks reflect the relevant Assessment Objectives.

A moderator, the representative of the Examination Board, will be assigned to approve the tasks that you have agreed with your teacher or to give advice when any changes need to be made to the tasks you have chosen. The total number of words that you will be asked to write for the two tasks together is between 2,000 and 2,500.

In this chapter we are going to:

- explore the opportunities offered by coursework for you to work in different ways

- look at each of the 10 prose texts (from which you will have to choose the two you want to study and write about in your coursework)

- explore the kinds of tasks that are appropriate in order to reflect the relevant Assessment Objectives

- look at the three drama texts (from which you will have to choose the one you want to study and write about in your coursework)

- explore the kinds of coursework tasks that are appropriate in order to reflect the Assessment Objectives.

Coursework – a different way of working

Your coursework will give you opportunities to work in ways that are very different from the way you would prepare for an exam. You will need to make the most of these opportunities in order to gain the maximum marks for your coursework. You will plan and write your coursework by working through the following stages, each of which gives you the opportunity to make the most of your work.

1 Negotiating the task

   Once you have chosen your two coursework texts, and you have read and studied them in detail, you will have time to think about **what particularly interests you** about the texts. Finding an appropriate **focus** for your writing is a crucial first step. Having taken it, you can then start to consider the kind of task you will negotiate with your teacher. Unlike the exam in Unit 1, where an examiner writes the questions, in the coursework you and your teacher are responsible for deciding the task. Of course, it must be constructed within the guidelines laid down by the Board, and we will look at those guidelines towards the end of this chapter.

2 Research

Once you have agreed your task with your teacher and it has been approved by the Exam Board moderator, you will have time and opportunity to carry out your own **research** on the topic you have chosen. You will need to organise yourself well and decide how you will keep the notes you take down in a systematic way so that they are of most use to you. You will, of course, need to keep a note of any sources that you consult, other than the primary text, as you will be expected to acknowledge these at the end of your essay.

3 Writing

When you are confident that you have done all the necessary reading and research, and have all the information that you require, you can turn to the actual writing of your essay. One advantage of writing coursework is that you can consult your teacher at any stage of the process. You will need to:

■ plan carefully

■ select the relevant material

■ organise and structure your writing

■ write the **first draft**.

You may wish to use the online planning tool to support the planning of your coursework.

You can, of course, show this **draft** to your teacher for comment, and you can then **redraft** your essay in the light of any advice or suggestions they give you.

4 Ensuring the quality of written communication and presentation

Your coursework gives you the opportunity to reconsider, rethink your ideas, and then draft and redraft your work. You will therefore be expected to present work that is well written, accurate and fluent, and well presented. If you choose to write your essays by hand, it is important that your writing is legible. If you choose to word-process your work (as most candidates do), it is important that you consider presentation and appearance. You should use a standard font that is clear and easy to read. You should use a font size no smaller than 12 points, and should not type your entire essay in italics or capitals.

🔍 The prose text

We are now going to look at each of the 10 prose texts from which you will be choosing one to study and write about in your coursework. The texts cover the period 1983 to 2003 – a fruitful 20-year time span in modern literature. Many of these texts have therefore been written during your lifetime. They all deal with social issues of identity in the 20th and 21st centuries, and eight of them are set during this time. The two exceptions are *Beloved* by Toni Morrison, which is set in the 1800s, and *The Handmaid's Tale* by Margaret Atwood, which is set in the future. Six of the novels are by female and four by male authors. With the exception of Angela Carter (*Wise Children*), each of these authors is alive at the time of writing this book. You will choose **one** of these texts and write a coursework essay on it.

We will consider the texts chronologically, in the order in which they were written.

1 *The Color Purple* by Alice Walker (1944–)

This novel was published in 1983.

Biography

Alice Walker was born to sharecropper parents in 1944 in Eatonton, Georgia, in the 'deep south' of the USA. After living in different American cities, she moved to California on the west coast. She said in an interview with *The Observer* in 2001:

> … I felt in Georgia and on the east coast generally very squeezed. People always want to keep you in a little box or they need to label you and fix you in time and location. I feel a greater fluidity here. People are much more willing to accept that nothing is permanent, everything is changeable so there is freedom and I do need to live where I can be free.

Her experiences of growing up in Georgia no doubt influenced her writing. The author of several novels, short stories, poetry collections and essays, she won the Pulitzer Prize and the American Book Award for *The Color Purple*. The novel was made into a successful box-office film by Steven Spielberg, with whom she worked closely on the screenplay.

In 1965, Walker met and later married Mel Leventhal, a Jewish civil rights lawyer. They became the first legally married interracial couple in Mississippi. This brought them a long battle with harassment, including death threats from the Ku Klux Klan. Later, in another flurry of publicity, she discussed her love affair with singer-songwriter Tracy Chapman in a December 2006 interview with the *Guardian*, explaining why they did not go public with their relationship, saying '… I was completely in love with her but it was not anybody's business but ours.'

Her political activism began in the 1960s during the civil rights movement, and she has since spoken publicly for the women's movement, the anti-apartheid movement, the anti-nuclear movement, and against female genital mutilation. Alice Walker started her own publishing company, Wild Trees Press, in 1984. You might catch her on a reading tour in the UK; that would be well worth your effort.

The story

The novel is set largely in the segregated, rural American south in the 1920s and 1930s, between World Wars One and Two. It focuses on the fortunes of Celie, a poor, uneducated, young black woman. At 14, she is sexually abused and becomes pregnant twice by a man she believes to be her father. After her children are taken away from her, she is forced to marry a widower and to look after his many children. In return, he systematically beats her. Separated from her beloved sister, Nettie, and deceived by her husband into believing that Nettie has lost all contact, it appears life could not get much worse.

Ironically, Celie gains strength from the two women who only come into her life as a result of her ugly marriage: Shug Avery, her husband's mistress, and Sofia, the wife of her husband's son. From this point, Celie begins to take control of her life and relationships. Eventually, after much painful struggle, Celie finds fulfilment and purpose. She becomes reunited with her sister, joyful in a sexual relationship with Shug, reconciled with her husband and successfully self-employed. She has even relocated her children and unravelled the mystery of her real father. Many of the characters also achieve positive outcomes. The ending, given the story, is a happy one.

Narrative viewpoint and structure

The story is told chronologically through a series of diary entries and letters. Initially, the diary entries are written by Celie and it is her viewpoint we are given. They are addressed to 'God' as letters. At this stage there is only one narrator. Later in the narrative, the story is told through 'actual' letters sent between Celie and her sister Nettie. At this point, there are two narrators, as we are given the viewpoints of both Celie and Nettie. All the narrative uses first person – although as diaries and letters, the technique of **direct address**, of addressing the reader as 'you', is often employed. Here there are two possible 'yous' – the character to whom the letter is written, and the reader of the novel itself. During this stage, Celie stops writing to God.

Use of the context of the struggle for identity

The novel draws on issues of:

- unequal racial identity, for African American descendants of slavery in a segregated society
- unequal female identity, particularly the low position of black women, mirroring actual concerns in society then and now
- solidarity and the identity of shared experience
- personal and financial independence as part of a person's identity.

All these issues of identity are concerned with the status of individuals within particular social groups.

2 *The Handmaid's Tale* by Margaret Atwood (1939–)

This novel was published in 1985.

Biography

Margaret Atwood was born and lives in Canada and is that country's most internationally famous novelist, poet and critic. As an activist she has demonstrated many times her commitment to social justice. Between 1984 and 1986, during the time she wrote and published *The Handmaid's Tale*, she was vice chairman of the Writers' Union of Canada, and president of International PEN, a group committed to promoting freedom of expression and freeing writers who are political prisoners. She also donated all of her Booker Prize money to environmental causes, and gave up her house in France after Jacques Chirac, the then French President, resumed nuclear testing. An active member of Amnesty International, Atwood once promised a free subscription to its bimonthly reports to the next person who said she was 'all doom and gloom'! She is often described as a feminist writer, as issues of gender sometimes appear prominently in her writing. Her work has also focused on Canadian national identity, Canada's relations with the United States and Europe, human rights and environmental issues.

The Handmaid's Tale won the first Arthur C. Clarke Award in 1987. This award acknowledges the novel's sub-genre as **science fiction**. Like many science-fiction novels, it is a **dystopia** and therefore paints a shocking society, which is undesirable and has broken away from the social norms that many in our society would currently accept.

The story

The novel is set in Cambridge, Massachusetts, USA in a more distant 21st century, ruled by Christian fundamentalism. It features a new society called the Republic of Gilead in which, after a revolution,

Commanders have taken control and many women, for no named reason, seem to be infertile. Fertile women have been wrenched from their lives, children and family to participate in a breeding project to repopulate the new world, which is in environmental disarray, yet is strictly socially controlled. Their new role, as handmaidens, is to mate with the Commanders under the supervision of their infertile wives. It is hinted that it is actually the men who are infertile due to environmental and chemical disasters, but the basis of the Gilead philosophy and power structure is that they cannot be criticised.

Offred (we are not told her 'real' name), the central character, is a handmaid, and the novel tells her story – of separation from her husband and child; of her placement with Commander Fred and his wife Serena Joy; of her dangerous and secret sexual relationship with the Commander's chauffeur, Nick; of memories of her life before; and of the fate of other women who are neither fertile nor socially acceptable to this new world.

The story climaxes ambiguously – Offred believes she is pregnant and is taken from the house one night in a raid. She is either caught for her relationship with Nick or freed by him and his underground friends. It is only when we read the 'Historical Notes' at the end that it is made clear she was helped to some kind of safety. The novel finishes with an even further future in which a professor is giving a lecture on the, by then defunct, Republic of Gilead, and we then learn that the story we have read has been relayed through him, from evidence gathered on tapes made by Offred after her time as a handmaid.

Narrative viewpoint and structure

There are 15 chapters, told in the first person, followed by the 'Historical Notes' at the end. Alternate chapters are entitled 'Night' (except Chapter 5) and often use **flashback**. The other alternate chapters narrate chronologically the 'present' events that Offred experiences. The 'Historical Notes' are narrated by Professor Pieixoto through **collective address**, signified by the use of 'we' towards his audience. His section, as a public lecture, is delivered in a **documentary** style, lending a type of **realism** to the novel and the events Offred narrates. Hence Atwood's choice of title for this section, 'Historical Notes'.

Use of the context of the struggle for identity

The obvious contexts are lost identity and controlled identity. This is revealed through an exploration of the social and historical contexts of women's social and economic exploitation, as well as women's relationships with each other and with men. The novel draws on the controversial ideas of subjugation and 'non-membership' of society, against a backdrop of a **totalitarian** (single ruling party) **theocratic** (religious-run) state. You will need to consider what parallels Atwood may be implying with the world of 1985, when the book was written, and our world now.

3 *Beloved* by Toni Morrison (1931–)

This novel was written in 1987.

Biography

Toni Morrison was born Chloe Anthony Wofford in 1931 in Ohio, USA to black sharecropper parents who moved there to escape the racism they had faced in the south. She is a teacher, editor and novelist, influenced by writers like James Baldwin and William Faulkner. Morrison has been a member of both the National Council on the Arts and the American Academy and Institute of Arts and Letters.

Beloved, her fifth novel, won the Pulitzer Prize for Fiction in 1988. Morrison made deserved history when she became the first black female author to be awarded the Nobel Prize for Literature in 1993. In 2001 she was named one of 'The 30 Most Powerful Women in America' by *Ladies' Home Journal*.

Morrison wrote *Beloved* at a time in her life when she had chosen to give up editing and to make her living from writing. She speaks of how this choice had made her feel free, which led her to contemplate, in her Foreword to the 2005 edition of the novel:

> … what 'free' could possibly mean to women. In the eighties, the debate was still roiling: equal pay, equal treatment, access to professions, schools … and choice without stigma. To marry or not. To have children or not. Inevitably these thoughts led me to the different history of black women in this country—a history in which marriage was discouraged, impossible, or illegal; in which birthing children was required, but 'having' them, being responsible for them—being, in other words, their parent—was as out of the question as freedom.

The story

The protagonist, Sethe, an escaped slave, tries to kill her four children to save them from slavery after her master catches up with her. She is successful only in murdering the unnamed infant, 'Beloved'. Sethe believes that her house, where she lives with her teenage daughter, Denver, is haunted by the dead baby daughter whose ghost has driven her brothers away out of fear. Paul D., whom Sethe knew in slavery, visits and manages to drive the ghost out for a while. However, this does not last and Beloved returns in many forms to take her place, even perhaps her revenge, in the family with Sethe, the mother whom she cannot let go. Eventually, after a harrowing series of events, the 'spell' breaks, and Beloved disappears. Paul D. returns to take care of a broken Sethe.

Narrative viewpoint and structure

This novel has a complex narrative structure and changing viewpoints. It begins with a chronological narrative of events in the 'present', told in the third person, largely from the viewpoint of the character of Sethe. It soon adopts the technique of flashback, using a first-person narrative. This highly personalised and intense first-person narrative is also used to represent the feelings of the three main female characters, Sethe, Denver and Beloved herself. The novel alternates between the third, and first-person narratives, with no warning or regularity in the narrative structure. The narrative overall is divided into three parts, but there is no other indication of how to 'break down' the story and the information it reveals. There are no chapter numbers or names, no contents page, no name given to each of the three parts.

Use of the context of the struggle for identity

Beloved is set in the mid 1800s, but is clearly a late 20th-century novel, with very modern ideas about the struggle for identity of its characters. It was in fact based on a true story, that of Margaret Garner, an escaped slave and young mother, who was arrested for killing one of her children and trying to kill the others rather than see them returned to slavery. Morrison was angry that Margaret Garner's tale had gone untold and that it was not considered a fitting subject for art.

There were, albeit rare, autobiographies about life as a slave woman, such as *Incidents in the Life of a Slave Girl* by Harriet Jacobs (1813–97) written and published, amazingly, in 1861, after Jacobs' escape from an obnoxious master. However, it would take another 126 years and many more atrocities before such a story, in the hands of this unsurpassed writer, would become a novel, *Beloved*, read the world over. This is reflected in Morrison's dedication in the front of the book, '*Sixty Million and more*'.

4 *Wise Children* by Angela Carter (1940–1992)

This novel was written in 1991.

Biography

Angela Carter was born in 1940, the daughter of English political radicals. According to Ali Smith, who wrote the Introduction to the 2006 edition of *Wise Children*, Carter 'was a committed feminist and socialist … .who saw all art as helplessly political, because made by history and belonging to its time.' Carter was, in her own words, 'the pure product of an advanced, industrialised, post-imperialist country in decline'.

Carter has defied her fiction being pigeon-holed.

A celebrated novelist for 30 years, *Wise Children* turned out to be Carter's last book. A year after its publication she died from cancer. She was a dear friend of the writer Salman Rushdie, and he wrote her obituary for the *Guardian* when she died in 1992, saying that she was a profound loss to fiction.

The story

In *Wise Children*, we sense the end of an era – the end of two sides of a long-standing theatrical family: the legitimate side, the Hazards, who perform highbrow drama; and the illegitimate side, the Chances, Dora and Nora, who act and sing in music hall chorus lines.

We are introduced to Dora (the narrator) and Nora (her twin sister). It becomes clear that Dora is writing her memoirs, and that this story is based on them. The story begins with the disappearance of Tiffany, a member of the sprawling Hazard/Chance dynasty. This prompts Dora into reminiscence. From here on in, we learn about their famous Shakespearean actor of a father, Melchior Hazard, and that they are his illegitimate children. Melchior has for years disowned Dora and Nora, claiming that they are his twin brother Perry's children. However, we are told that Melchior slept with the chambermaid 'Pretty Kitty' during World War One and that she died after childbirth. Her landlady, 'Grandma' Chance, took the children in as her own, and from there grows the story of these twins. For a twist, there is some debate as to whether she is in actual fact the mother and Kitty was just a fabrication. The name Chance is already an apt moniker for the two girls. The unclear origins of Dora and Nora and the carnival backdrop set the scene for some **suspension of disbelief**. We follow their fortunes, ending, after the loss of Grandma Chance and some spectacular recounting of theatrical tales, in Chapter 5, with their attendance at the 100th birthday party of their now acknowledged father.

Narrative viewpoint and structure

The novel is written in the first person with one narrator, Dora, who uses direct address to talk to the reader in a chatty, **vernacular** and sometimes vulgar style. The mood and genre are comic; the setting is London. The story unfolds initially across a day in Chapter 1; in Chapters 2 to 4 it then recalls the events of several decades and the lives of the twins, Nora and Dora; in the final Chapter 5 we re-enter the 'present'.

The novel is divided into five chapters, like a five-act play for the stage. Its structure mirrors the structure of a play, with the use of a chaotic, messy Chapter 3 in which uncontrollable events spiral out of the characters' hands, like the often equally chaotic Act 3 in Shakespeare's comedies. The novel even concludes with the play script convention of a character list, a dramatis personae, and makes reference to the stage, song and dance in the last line.

Use of the context of the struggle for identity

Critics have struggled to impose labels and sub-genres onto Carter's work as it spans so many forms and ideas. It has been said that she is a **magic realist**, in her use of time, fantasy and horror, and that she rejects **realism**. However, she scoffed at these attempts to define her, believing that 'realism' is not the only way of being or communicating what is real. Clearly, her fiction, and even this novel which actually makes limited use of the fantasy and magic narratives that she employed in her earlier novels, explores a very different reality to the **realism** we find in the novels considered so far.

5 *Snow Falling on Cedars* by David Guterson (1956–)

This novel was published in 1994.

Biography

David Guterson was born in Seattle in 1956 and now lives on Bainbride Island in Puget Sound, USA. He is an American author and magazine journalist, formerly a high school English teacher. He has five children, all of whom he taught himself at home. He explains why in his book *Family Matters: Why Homeschooling Makes Sense* (1992). Guterson said of his father that 'One of the things I heard [from him] early on was to find something you love to do – before you think about money or anything else. The other thing was to do something that you feel has a positive impact on the world.'

In *Snow Falling on Cedars*, Guterson has developed his ideas about the moral function of literature. He said in an interview that 'Fiction writers shouldn't dictate to people what their morality should be … Yet not enough writers are presenting moral questions for reflection, which I think is a very important obligation.'

He has written novels and short stories. *Snow Falling on Cedars* was his first novel. However, in 2001 it became one of the targets of B.R. Myers' *A Reader's Manifesto*. A damning analysis of contemporary American literary fiction, Myers claims this novel is pretentious and not very good. Not everyone agreed. It won the 1995 PEN/Faulkner Award.

The story

It is 1954 in San Piedro, a tiny fishing island off the north-west Pacific coast of the USA, recovering from the blows of the World War Two 10 years before. It is winter and freezing, and a local fisherman, the German American Carl Heine, has been found dead on his boat, presumed murdered. Very quickly, the Japanese American Kabuo Miyamoto, also a local fisherman, is arrested, imprisoned and put on trial for murder. The story takes place across a matter of weeks, but covers the events of a few decades – life on the island before the war, the war, life on the island since the war, right up to the trial itself.

Ishmael Chambers is the island's Jewish American journalist, who is covering the trial for his local newspaper. His role is complicated by the fact that, before the war, he was involved romantically with a Japanese American woman, Hatsue, who became Kabuo's wife. This is complicated further by the fact that he is still in love with an utterly unattainable Hatsue, who is devastated by the trial of her husband.

We are told early on how all three men grew up together and that each of them is a veteran soldier of the war, when all of them fought on the side of America.

Narrative viewpoint and structure

The novel has a very complex narrative structure, making use of the novel's sub-genre of **detective thriller**. It is written in the third person and gives different character viewpoints, depending on whose perspective the author wants us to consider, like weighing up evidence. The novel is divided into 32 chapters. There is an overarching, forward-moving, chronological narrative of a trial and its conclusion for all the characters affected by the outcome.

This overarching narrative is interspersed with non-chronological memories and recollections, conversations and cross-examination, to fill in all the aspects of the past that inform the events in the 'present'. These details are presented to us within and across several of the chapters. The novel concludes in Chapters 30–32, which wrestle with what it means to 'do the right thing', however hard that may feel. This ensures the appropriate outcome for the trial, the novel and the relationship between the characters and you, the reader.

The novel offers a sort of justice but no happiness, and the mood is often melancholic and even heartbreaking. Despite this, and its wartime subject matter, it is a breathtakingly beautiful novel; a love story, where we are encouraged to engage sympathetically with many characters.

Use of the context of the struggle for identity

The novel deals with anti-Japanese racism directed towards the defendant Kabuo, whose family has lived in America for generations. The attitudes are presumed to be caused by the dreadful and terrifying American experience of World War Two battles, most notably at Pearl Harbor and Okinawa, which was in turn answered with the horrific and devastating American nuclear bombing of Hiroshima and Nagasaki. Guterson writes about the attitudes and effects of racism from the past, suggesting that there might be parallels within the society from which he writes.

6 *The Woman Who Walked into Doors* by Roddy Doyle (1958–)

This novel was published in 1996.

Biography

Roddy Doyle was born in Dublin in 1958. He was a teacher in his old school, where his students inspired his self-published first novel, *The Commitments*. He did not give up teaching until the day *Paddy Clarke Ha Ha Ha* came out. Doyle opens his novel *Paddy Clarke Ha Ha Ha* with a nodding tribute to his Dublin predecessor James Joyce, whose development of the narrative style of the **stream of consciousness** cannot have been far from Doyle's mind when he later wrote *The Woman Who Walked into Doors*.

The Woman Who Walked into Doors features a fictional heroine named Paula Spencer, who is the same heroine of his follow-up novel, *Paula Spencer* (2007), his only first-person narrator and his greatest depiction of dignity despite degradation.

The story

The plot is short and simple. Paula grows up an average girl, nothing to make you worry, other than the lack of opportunities for working-class Dubliners like her. She meets and marries, with the disapproval of her father, Charlo Spencer, an attractive, rough diamond who turns to small-time crime. Paula becomes pregnant on the honeymoon, and a few months later Charlo begins a lifetime of violence against his young and vulnerable wife. Their families seem to fade away. Paula never mentions friends, and the hospital doctors, who know her well, never ask how she receives her life-threatening injuries.

This narrative stretches out before the reader without hope or change, until the day Paula sees that her eldest daughter, now 18, is in danger from Charlo, her father. This galvanises in Paula a strength and courage that Charlo has never seen. She retaliates and it drives him away. Her elder son, however, leaves also, as he blames his mother and not his father. That is the only sense he can muster from all he has seen. The story shows how Paula then attempts to salvage a life for her family from the ruins, deal with her alcoholism and earn a living.

The final event of the novel, Charlo's unrelated death, which is implied from the first page, seems little more than a deserved sorry end, rather than the release for Paula which we yearn for throughout the novel. The story shows us that, by the end, she has released herself.

Narrative viewpoint and structure

If you read the sections on *Beloved* and *Snow Falling on Cedars*, you will have been introduced already to the ideas of a complex and multilayered narrative structure. *The Woman who Walked into Doors* pushes the boundaries even further in its use of time, place, memory and recollection. The narrative style and the subject matter are inseparable. Doyle pushes us into the nightmare of the heroine's life and we see what she sees, we know what she knows, we process and understand what she understands. Even though the events at the end of the novel are delivered at the beginning, we make no more sense of them than the character Paula herself. It is only when we are made to do what Doyle has her do – sit down and trace them, however haphazardly, however repeatedly, in whatever order – that the jigsaw finally emerges with its pieces in the right places.

Use of the context of the struggle for identity

This novel draws heavily on the idea of **catharsis**, a dramatic technique from tragedy, which demands a purging of the reader's emotions through experiencing, in a kind of real-time, the sufferings and redemption of the central character. This is a literary context, but it has repercussions for the social context in which the novel was written. We see that the most impressive act of catharsis is the one achieved by the writer himself, Roddy Doyle.

To convey the experience of abuse to the point where the readers comprehend the terror for themselves is craft enough; that it is a tale of abuse of women, communicated in this most personal of styles, by a man, is an act of total sympathy, of understanding. For this alone, Doyle follows a tradition made great by the European and British Victorian male **representational** novelists like Thomas Hardy, Charles Dickens, Emile Zola, Gustav Flaubert and Leo Tolstoy. Through **social realism**, we experience the trials suffered by downtrodden women, who are not *even entitled* to an identity, crushed by poverty or confined by cruelty; in Paula's case, both.

7 *Hullabaloo in the Guava Orchard* by Kiran Desai (1971–)

This novel was published in 1998.

Biography

Kiran Desai was born in 1971 in Delhi, India, where she lived until she was 14. She spent a year in England and then moved to the USA. She still revisits the family home in Delhi every year. She is the daughter of the distinguished Anglo-Indian writer Anita Desai. *Hullabaloo in the Guava Orchard* is her first novel and it won the Betty Trask Award, a prize given by the Society of Authors for the best new novels by citizens of the Commonwealth of Nations under the age of 35. Her second novel, *The Inheritance of Loss*, won the 2006 prestigious Man Booker Prize and the National Book Critics Circle Fiction Award.

The story

Hullabaloo in the Guava Orchard is a very funny blend of the real emotions of characters and the ridiculous scenarios of a backwater town which reinvents itself as a busy and important place. The source for this blend is our hero, Sampath Chawla, an aimless middle-class post office clerk, who tries to escape his pointless and unsuccessful life by climbing a guava tree to shake off domestic and social pressures. He gains recognition as a hermit and the guava orchard becomes the epicentre of all the characters.

The 'hullabaloo' begins when everyone – from his family, to the people of Shahkot town, the police and even the monkeys who live in the trees – tries to make purpose and importance out of an otherwise whimsical and irrelevant act of occupation of a guava tree. Through this they seek self-purpose and self-importance.

Sampath, the good-for-nothing daydreamer of a clerk, had previously spent his time in the post office reading other people's mail. Now, from his on-high position, he is able to give back to them details and opinions on things he ought not to know. This leads to his guru status and people start referring to him as 'Baba', meaning saint. When the monkeys move in, he is renamed 'Monkey Baba'. Of course, Sampath's smugness and his artificial, groundless status cannot last. The townspeople's attempts to free their guru from the monkey invasion paradoxically lead to his downfall, in more ways than one …

Narrative viewpoint and structure

The book is written in 25 chapters. The narrative is chronological. The story is told in the third person. The focus is the character of Sampath, but he is only one of a tableau of credible and sympathetic characters, starting with his family. The setting is the small town of Shahkot. Chapter 1 recalls the situation in which Sampath was born, to set the scene for events that follow. From there, we are taken through the novel in an uninterrupted linear order of time and events.

There are no subplots, complex narratives, shifting viewpoints or radical language techniques. There are no historical references, no specific intertextuality. There are no distractions from the chronological narrative. In the case of this novel, the transparent narrative style is its success, making it a very accessible read.

Use of the context of the struggle for identity

The use of animals as a device and the symbolism of the weather are keys to the fortunes of the characters and the progression of the plot.

This provides a particular and recognisable focus for modern novels set in India and the Indian subcontinent that present aspects of Indian cultural, geographical and religious identities; this is the social context of struggles for identity in this novel.

The novel is a **satire**, because it challenges society's willingness to find a spiritual leader, irrespective of suitability on every level, and turn them unwittingly into a god. However, despite its satirical style, Desai is not mocking India itself, either as a concept or a place. She says, 'I think my first book was filled with all that I loved most about India and knew I was in the inevitable process of losing.' The affection in her writing is evidence of this.

It is hard to ignore comparisons between this novel and society's current and hollow obsession with empty celebrity. The (self-)elevation of people who are 'famous for being famous', creations of media sensation, is a striking context for the creation of the hullabaloo that occurs, in this case, in a guava tree. Additionally, comparisons can be drawn with how we treat actual celebrities, who are famous because of their exceptional talent, from Elvis to Georgie Best. The untimely deaths of these proper superstars will still choke generations of admirers, yet it has long been acknowledged that it was their celebrity that killed them. This sober thought can provide a useful framework to consider the novel as an exploration of stolen identity, when the individual – in this case Sampath – is lost beyond all recognition to an 'image'.

8 *Trumpet* by Jackie Kay (1961–)

This book was published in 1998.

Biography

Jackie Kay was born in 1961 in Edinburgh, to a Scottish mother and a Nigerian father. She was adopted by a white couple at birth and was brought up in Glasgow, Scotland. The experience of being adopted by and growing up within a white family inspired her first collection of poetry, *The Adoption Papers* (1991). The poems deal with an adopted child's search for a cultural identity, which is told through three different voices: an adoptive mother, a birth mother and a daughter.

This paved the way for her first novel, *Trumpet*, seven years later. The novel echoes the poetry's subject matter of adoption and the search for personal and cultural identity. The use of three main narrative voices also recalls the style of the poetry collection. *Trumpet* was awarded the *Guardian* Fiction Prize.

The story was created following Kay's interest in a newspaper obituary she read on the life of musician Billy Tipton, whose complete identity was only revealed after death. It also reflects Kay's love of jazz, which she has also explored in a biography of the late, great black American jazz singer Bessie Smith.

The story

The novel tells the story of Scottish jazz trumpeter Joss Moody, whose death revealed that he was, in fact, a woman. His wife, Millicent Moody, had always known this. His adopted son Colman had not. There are four main stories here:

■ the life of the trumpeter himself
■ the grief and love felt for him by his wife

- the shock and turmoil of discovery felt by his son
- the reactions of friends, acquaintances, strangers and professionals – doctors, registrars, undertakers, the tabloid press, the music industry – to the news that Joss Moody was born a woman.

The story is told as a journey which the son, Colman Moody, must take. The narrative traces how he comes to terms with his father's complete identity and how he handles that in public and around people he loves. The narrative presents how he then develops his own identity as a result.

The presentation of the grieving wife has no such journey to take. She and her husband have clear identities, as individuals and as a couple, about which she has no struggle. Her journey is that of any widow: the burden of sorrow. That she has to endure the larger social consequences of his death simply compounds her loss and loneliness.

The third journey we are told is that of the tabloid journalist, Sophie Stone, who travels the country preying on Colman, his mother and everyone who had any contact with the dead trumpeter, flashing money to lure her targets.

The conclusion of the novel shows Colman reunited with his mother, his father and himself. It shows the tabloid journalist for what she is.

Narrative viewpoint and structure

Kay develops the narrative principally through the voices of Moody's wife, his adopted son and a journalist from a tabloid newspaper. These voices are supported by a larger cast of characters described in the story above. We also hear from Joss himself, both in death and in a letter to his son, meaning that every perspective – social and personal, sympathetic and unsympathetic, the man and the musician – is communicated to the reader.

The novel employs a complex **split narrative** structure. Different stories are told chronologically for both the mother and the son, with some use of flashback in each case. It is told chronologically for the journalist. It is told as anecdotes by the rest of the characters, including Joss himself. It has documentary-style sections, like 'Obituaries' and 'Editorial'.

There are 32 sections, all significantly named. Many of these section titles, for example 'House and Home' and 'Good Hotels', appear several times. Patterns of use are established for each section name. For example, 'House and Home' gives us the first-person voice of the wife in the 'present' and in recollection; 'Good Hotels' offers us the third-person voice of her son as he makes his literal and emotional journey. However, sometimes the pattern breaks or shifts to signify either a change in attitude, as in the presentation of the son's acceptance of the facts; or a change in location, as in the son's appearance at the mother's house; or a change in relationship, as in the sections where the son becomes disenchanted with the journalist.

Use of the context of the struggle for identity

Kay's own identity, as a black, Scottish, adopted, lesbian woman living in England, suggests she has a lot to tell us about the search for identity, both socially and personally. Kay uses stories developed from memoirs or newspaper reports to tell a tale that needs to be told, of a social group whose identity has had no recognised expression, no voice. It also allows Kay to tell a tale of social realism about people and lived experience that some would find hard to believe. Clearly, we are dealing with the idea of forbidden identity in this novel.

Kay's identity as a poet is clear in the language of the novel – she writes, like the poet Maya Angelou in her prose works, a beautiful, rich poetic narrative. The novel's strength and grace lie in the description of her characters, rather than in the narrative structure – which some may feel is a little over-complex for its subject matter.

9 *Spies* by Michael Frayn (1933–)

This novel was published in 2002.

Biography

Michael Frayn was born in London in 1933 and started as a journalist on the *Guardian* and *Observer* newspapers. He is a rare example of a dramatist whose novels are equally accomplished. He is also a translator of Russian classic plays.

Spies won the Whitbread novel award and the 2003 Commonwealth Writers Prize.

The story

Spies is the tale of two pubescent boys whose adventures and imaginations overpower their reason and reality one summertime during World War Two, in a quiet and respectable English suburb. From the moment that the socially conscious, lower middle-class only child Keith Hayward fancifully tells Stephen Wheatley, his less wealthy, less confident, less egocentric neighbourhood friend, that 'My mother is a German spy', the two boys invent a narrative fantasy which spirals out of control.

Undertaking an amateur but documented surveillance of Keith's mother, the greatest fuel to their invented fire is the discovery that she is taking provisions on secret visits to nearby abandoned countryside. The boys assume it is for a German soldier, possibly a downed pilot, and their lives revolve around a mission to uncover the mystery. Meanwhile, Keith's Uncle Peter is serving as a pilot in the British Royal Air Force, involved in bombing raids over Germany. Interlaced with this fantasy, as real as their own lives to the boys, is Stephen's emerging teenage self, of smoking, kissing girls and irritating elder brothers. This groundedness gives the young Stephen a hold on reality that Keith does not have. This link to the world around him and the obedient subservience he demonstrates to adults, and even to Keith, prompts Keith's mother to use him as her confidant in a dangerous game of clandestine liaisons. As secrets are uncovered – by Keith's father, the neighbours, the police – Keith's mother, Keith and Stephen must face the consequences of their various actions. Needless to say, the 'spy' of the novel is not this housewife, and there are no Germans in the woods.

However, the truths that the novel reveals are far less palatable than Keith or even Stephen can accept. We see Stephen as an old man, long out of contact with Keith and the neighbourhood, return to the street to relive the past and its story, and to demonstrate his understanding of the events and issues they raised half a century before.

Narrative viewpoint and structure

The novel is written in the first person and the character of Stephen is the narrator throughout. The story is structured as a **bildungsroman**, with the central character going on a journey of self-discovery through revisiting the memories of childhood as an adult. You need to consider the use of symbolism in conveying this self-discovery in the novel, particularly that of gardens and plants.

For the most part it is a chronological narrative divided into 11 chapters, switching between present and flashbacks. The interesting aspect of this novel, regarding structure and viewpoint, is that it is written largely in the present tense. Where it shifts to the more conventional use of the past tense is in the episodes where Stephen is in his 'present' as an adult, either detailing 'current events' or recalling past ones. Where Stephen deals with events from the past, in the flashback of the novel, the narrative is in the present tense. Michael Frayn is a dramatist who writes fiction. His use of the present tense is linked to his experience of writing play scripts, consisting mainly of dialogue, for a live audience. How does this language technique help him to present the emerging identities of teenage boyhood?

Use of the context of the struggle for identity

Identity in crisis is a feature of this novel. We have a boy who thinks his mother is a spy because his own life lacks creative depth. We have a mother who is unfulfilled in marriage and domesticity and seeks love beyond acceptable margins. Concealed identity is also a feature, with almost every character hiding or hiding from something.

The social context of World War Two is obviously a key to the novel. The country is at war. There are enemies and there are allies. There are us and them, right and wrong. There is a chance to be a hero or a coward, for honour and sacrifice or selfish desire. These are the moral judgements which the historical world of the novel would make on each character, and these are the ideals and ideas which would have dominated the culture of the time. As well as the instinctual paranoia of wartime Britain, there is the context of a hypocritical, domestic, status-seeking society. You can ask yourself how relevant they are to us today and how Frayn presents these contextual influences in the novel. Remember also that these larger questions on life are filtered through the half-knowing eyes of children.

10 *Vernon God Little* by DBC Pierre (1961–)

This novel was published in 2003.

Biography

The best snapshot biography of DBC Pierre can be found inside the cover of the 2004 Faber paperback edition:

> Born in Australia DBC Pierre spent a lavish upbringing in Mexico learning the tools of his undoing. He undid himself on three continents during his twenties, spending his thirties in London and the West Indies. Having plied a piecemeal trade since childhood as designer, photographer, film-maker and cartoonist, his first novel, Vernon God Little, erupted just before his fortieth birthday. It went on to win the MAN Booker Prize, the Whitbread Best First Novel Award and the Bollinger Everyman Wodehouse Award for Comic Writing in 2003.
>
> A British citizen, Pierre now lives halfway up a small mountainside in Ireland, where he plans to write more books.

This biography does not tell you two interesting facts:

■ 2007 sees this award-winning first novel adapted for the London stage.
■ Born **Peter Warren Finlay**, the 'DBC' part of his *nom de plume* stands for 'Dirty But Clean'. 'Pierre' was a childhood nickname copying a cartoon character of that name.

The story

Vernon Gregory Little is a 15-year-old boy living unhappily with his mother in Martirio, Texas, nearer to Mexico than mainstream USA. One disastrous and sweltering summer, he is accused of murdering his classmates and teacher in a shooting spree with his friend Jesus Navarro, who died in the incident, leaving Vernon as the fall guy for all the deaths. As the novel progresses, Vernon finds he cannot escape the accusation, which he denies. However, as he is utterly unable to convince authority figures, from the law to the school and his family, his situation escalates dangerously.

Meanwhile, his mother takes up with Eulalio Ledesma, a shady man who appears in town, claiming to work for a TV news channel. 'Lally', as he is known, becomes instrumental in Vernon's destruction. Lost, Vernon eventually runs out of options and, facing multi-murder charges, absconds to Mexico. Controlled by burgeoning sexual feelings, he adds hurdles to his freedom with his desire for an unreachable young woman.

Accused now of virtually every murder reported, the novel and Vernon's life take on a surreal and fantastic quality when he is captured and convicted. Presented as incredible but frighteningly believable, the inmates of death row are televised, and each week the viewers vote for who they want to kill or keep. It is at this point that our hero becomes Vernon God Little.

Narrative viewpoint and structure

The book is divided into five parts, named 'Acts', with a total of 27 chapters.

The story is told in the first person from Vernon's perspective, using colloquial and conversational language, including swearing. The character of Vernon is one who may not necessarily elicit sympathy initially, but is likely to by the novel's end. It is a clear chronological depiction of the feelings that affect Vernon as he journeys through events and places, with some use of recollection to fill in any relevant knowledge gaps for the reader.

Use of the context of the struggle for identity

The outcome resolves every narrative problem the novel raises – the question of Vernon's struggle for identity, typically that of many young, vulnerable men trying to grow up and understand the world they inhabit. What the novel cannot solve so easily are the contexts of wider social problems that it highlights – American (youth) gun culture, media intrusion into privacy, the cult of 'reality TV' and, like *Hullabaloo in the Guava Orchard*, our obsession with fake celebrities. It also criticises our reliance on fast food, advertising, shopping, especially for domestic, status-driven trivia, and, most crucially, trial by media. It suggests that these behaviours are shallow and damaging to human dignity. All these contexts suggest social and personal identity in crisis. This is perhaps the 'Presence of Death' in the subtitle.

■ Writing about your chosen novel

Having reviewed all the possible choices, we are going to turn to the writing of the essay.

1 Studying the text

You will need to read your chosen novel several times so that you know and understand the text, and can analyse and explore the ways the writer's choices of structure and language shape your response.

You will need to consider, discuss and make notes on the following aspects of the text:

- the writer's purposes
- the structure of the novel
- the narrative viewpoint
- interesting aspects of language and imagery
- key themes
- characters.

2 Finding a focus for your essay

When you know your novel well, with your teacher's help you will need to find an aspect of the text that interests you and about which you can construct an appropriate task. An appropriate task might focus on any of the aspects that you were invited to consider in the previous paragraph.

Your teacher will help you to construct a task that enables you to:

- write an informed and relevant response to your text using coherent and accurate written expression (AO1)
- show that you can analyse the ways the writer's choices of structure and language shape meaning (AO2)
- explore your interpretation of the text (AO3)
- show your understanding of how the text reflects the context of 'The Struggle for Identity in Modern Literature' (AO4).

3 Interpretation or transformation?

Here you have another choice to make. For this essay you can:

either

- write a conventional essay that explores some aspect of the text like characterisation, theme or structure, with a focus on your **personal informed interpretation** of the text

or

- produce a piece of **creative, transformational** writing, such as an alternative ending, a 'missing' chapter, a letter from or diary of a character in the novel. This piece will be assessed against the same Assessment Objectives as a more conventional essay, so it will need to reflect the writer's style, the way characters are realised, and so on.

Here are some suggestions as to how you might approach each of these options.

■ **Activity**

Write as many tasks as you can on the aspect of your chosen text that interests you. You can do this individually, with a partner or in a group. You can then share your tasks with your partner or the group, and get your teacher to check that they are appropriate.

■ **Activity**

Think of as many ways as you can of writing a creative, transformational task for your chosen novel. You can do this individually, with a partner or in a group. You can then share your ideas and discuss them with your teacher.

The personal informed interpretation

■ If your choice of novel were *Beloved* by Toni Morrison, an appropriate task might be:
'An exploration of the ways Toni Morrison presents the character of Sethe.'

■ Or, if you had chosen *Trumpet* by Jackie Kay, it might be:
'Explore the ways Kay portrays sexual identity in *Trumpet*.'

■ Or, if you had chosen *Wise Children* by Angela Carter, it might be:
'Examine the structure of *Wise Children* and assess the impact of the structure on the ways you interpret and respond to the book.'

■ Or, if you had chosen *Vernon God Little* by DBC Pierre, it might be:
'Explore the effects of Pierre's choice of narrator on the ways you interpret the novel.'

The creative, transformational piece

This is your opportunity to move out from the actual text and to create your own piece of writing. But remember that your writing needs to have developed from the text and to read as though it could be an integral part of it.

■ If you had chosen to study *Snow Falling on Cedars* by David Guterson, you could write The Epilogue, for example from the viewpoint of either Hatsue or Kabuo.

■ If you were studying *The Color Purple* by Alice Walker, you could compose Shug's or Mr __.'s diary.

🔍 The drama text

Now we will turn to the second piece of writing in the coursework folder, and begin by looking at the choices for the drama text.

There is a choice of three drama texts set for study in this coursework unit, and you will be studying **one** of them. These are the choices, in order of the time of composition:

1 *Death and the King's Horseman* by Wole Soyinka (1934–)

This play was first published in 1975 and performed in Nigeria in 1976, directed by Soyinka.

Biography

Wole Soyinka was born in in 1934 in western Nigeria, where he grew up. He came to England as a young man to study at Leeds University. He developed an interest in politics and by the 1960s was involved in attempts to overthrow the Nigerian government on claims of corruption and violence in the midst of strikes and civil uprising. This led to his imprisonment in 1967. Released in 1969, by 1971 Soyinka had gone into self-exile from Nigeria.

When a coup overthrew the government of Nigeria in 1975, Soyinka returned to a professorship there and *Death and the King's Horseman* was published. However, this reconciliation did not last and he was soon critical of the new power-bearers. In 1997, after several changes of government, his relationship with Nigerian officialdom ended again in exile. He was charged with treason and placed on trial in his absence.

Throughout his career as a dramatist and political activist, he has worked tirelessly to uncover and publicise inequality, corruption and brutality, particularly – but not only – in his country.

In 1986 he was awarded the Nobel Prize for Literature. Believed by many to be Africa's most important dramatist, he is a prolific and influential writer, constantly on tour and giving lectures.

The play

Death and the King's Horsemen is set in 1944 in Oyo, an ancient Yoruba city in Nigeria.

Elesin is the King's chief Horseman. After a life of luxury in this privileged role, it is his duty to follow the King in death by committing ritual suicide. Flawed by pride and ego, he is reluctant to leave the material world he has enjoyed, even managing to fit in a consummated marriage as he prepares for his death. This delay allows the British military to catch up with him, condemning, as Christians, the immorality of his plan. His arrest prevents his fulfilment of the ritual and leaves him, rejected, in eternal shame in this life and beyond.

Fig. 3.1 *Wole Soyinka*

The cultural setting is colonial Nigeria, where the British rule *in situ*. There are five scenes with alternate settings of place the play begins in the streets and marketplace (the African Yoruban world), moves to the house of the British District Officer (the colonial world), returns to the marketplace, and then to the British Residency. It ends in a collaboration of settings the King's Horseman (Yoruban) in prison (colonial). The play is a tragedy.

The time frame of the action is not specified but feels continuous, and the play is designed to run without an interval. Stage directions are brief, but Soyinka is overt in his characterisation. Despite the setting, he wants the spiritual and personal aspects of the tragedy of the King's Horseman to be emphasised, and the colonial angle minimised as a catalyst of events only. The play has much to say about honour, duty and ritual.

> ■ **Did you know?**
>
> The Methuen Student Edition of this text is excellent and includes every possible support for your literary study and contextual understanding, including an interview with Soyinka.

Use of the context of the struggle for identity

This is a play written 30 years after it is set. It focuses on cultural identity under threat and the responsibilities of personal and communal identity. It is based on the real-life identical events in 1945. Names are changed and the drama explores more than biographical details.

Soyinka draws on traditions of music, dance and storytelling from African theatre. He is also influenced by the playwright Bertolt Brecht (see Chapter 6), sharing similar political ideals and using some of Brecht's theatrical devices. As his biography shows, Soyinka is educated in the theatre of Shakespeare and the Greeks, and has been criticised by some Africans for his use of Western literary models.

2 *Top Girls* by Caryl Churchill (1938–)

This play was first published in 1982 and performed at the Royal Court Theatre in London.

Biography

Caryl Churchill was born in London in 1938, grew up in Canada and returned to England as a student, where she has worked since. She has written several plays over the past 50 years. *Top Girls*, written halfway through this illustrious career, is possibly her most famous.

Labelled as a feminist, socialist playwright, her radical politics are mirrored by her radical dramatic style. Experimental and innovative, she had very modern ideas about theatre as social commentary and was involved with the rise in socialist theatre promoted by the Royal Court Theatre in the 1960s and 1970s. This style focuses on characters and action as socially significant rather than as psychological explorations of individual people and situations. Identity, then, is always treated as a communal rather than an individual matter, with characters used as vehicles to convey the message. *Top Girls* is such a play.

The play

Its focus is the meeting of several female characters: (i) five women from the past transcend history (be it from the world of art, religion or literary) to represent different eras and lifestyles but the same social concern the subjugation of women through the ages; (ii) the women working for the employment agency, Top Girls, and their families.

Act One focuses on Marlene, whose promotion to managing director of the agency causes resentment in the male characters, which we see later, and is celebrated by Marlene at a restaurant meal with the women from the past. The play champions women's generally denied right to exist and flourish as separate from men, with neither support by or for them.

Fig. 3.2 *Still from a production of* Top Girls

The setting of the play is early 1980s London, in Thatcherite Britain: Act One, a restaurant; Act Two, an office and a backyard; Act Three, a kitchen. The settings range between domestic and professional. Traditionally female or traditionally male, each environment here is dominated by the women in the play.

Use of the context of the struggle for identity

The play does not suggest that the female characters are better, easier or nicer people than the men. These are the same ideas explored by the poet Carol Ann Duffy in her poetry collection on your exam text list, *The World's Wife*. The play also explores the social class structure which is supported by many women and makes them divided amongst themselves, as the opening scene with the waitress in the restaurant shows.

The inspiration and context for the play is clearly Churchill's view of the social inequality of female identity and experience. Also influenced by Bertolt Brecht (see Chapter 6), Churchill uses the obvious theatricality of 'walk-on performances' from women across history to communicate her larger social concerns. Yet this use of history, like Brecht's, reveals very contemporary truths. Here, they support Churchill's political ideas of a common experience between many women, wherever and whenever they live.

The play highlights Churchill's belief in the mistake made in believing that a female prime minister could represent women's liberation. Churchill's point is that emancipation could not come from such a right-wing, class-ridden and patriarchal philosophy as that which ruled 1980s Britain. The focus on women's unchanging experience and the universal use of female character highlight these contradictions.

3 *Making History* by Brian Friel (1929–)

This play was first published in 1989 and performed in 1988 in Derry.

Biography

Brian Friel was born in County Tyrone in 1929 and has written several key dramas which continue an unparalleled tradition of realism in 20th-century Irish theatre. He is part of the 'theatre of ideas' and has frequently developed dramas exploring Irish identity. In 1980 he formed the touring theatre company, Field Day, with the Irish actor Stephen Rea.

The play

Making History, although set at the end of the 16th century, is not a historical drama, in that it is not a play about the distant past. This play has only four scenes and six characters. A play dealing with such a large-scale social and political event – a battle and its consequences – suggests that the characters themselves represent something much wider than their own actions in the play.

The tragedy is not that of a character, nor even that of the central one, Hugh O'Neill. As in O'Casey's Dublin plays, the tragedy belongs to Ireland and the sacrifice of Irish identity. The historical pivot for this sacrifice is presented in the play as the Battle of Kinsale between Ireland and England.

The drama is divided into two acts: act 1, before the battle, the time of promise and hope; Act 2, after the battle, the time of betrayal and despair.

Fig. 3.3 *Still from a production of* Making History

Use of the context of the struggle for identity

Like Brecht, in the play *Mother Courage and her Children* (1940) (see Chapter 6), Friel has used history, a historical battle, to reveal contemporary truths about the tragedy and causes of divided identity in Irish society.

However, unlike Bertolt Brecht and Caryl Churchill, and like his compatriot Sean O'Casey (see Chapter 6), Friel has used the theatre of **social realism** to depict characters and settings of credible and close realistic detail to engage the audience's sympathy for the fallen heroes of the play.

Friel rewinds to a time when religion was not the central concern, to expose the political colonial roots of the present situation and the 20th-century apartheid that developed. Friel's bleak conclusion sheds light on drama written before and since on the ongoing struggle for Irish identity, here dramatised as a struggle lost hundreds of years before.

■ Writing about the chosen drama text

Having reviewed the three possible choices of drama texts, we will now turn to a consideration of the kind of task you need to construct.

1 Studying the text

You will need to read your chosen drama text several times so that you know and understand the text, and can explore and analyse the ways the writer's choices of structure and language shape your responses.

You will need to consider, discuss and make notes on the following aspects of the text:

■ the writer's purposes

■ the structure and the setting of the play

■ interesting aspects of language

■ key themes

■ characters.

2 Finding a focus for your essay

When you know your chosen play well, with your teacher's help you will need to find an aspect of the text that interests you and about which you can construct an appropriate task. An appropriate task might focus on any of the aspects that you were invited to consider in the previous paragraph.

Your teacher will help you to construct a task which enables you to:

■ write an informed and relevant response to your text using coherent and accurate written expression (AO1)

■ show that you can analyse the ways the writer's choices of structure and language shape meaning (AO2)

■ explore your interpretation of the text and make connections with other texts (AO3)

■ show your understanding of how the text reflects the context of the struggle for identity (AO4).

3 Comparison with the prose text or connection to other plays about the struggle for identity

Here you have another choice to make. For this essay, you can:

either

■ place the chosen play in its dramatic context, reaching out to your wider reading in plays about the struggle for identity

or

■ connect the chosen play to the chosen prose text.

Whichever task you choose, you will focus on aspects of the drama text such as theme, structure or characterisation.

■ If the two chosen texts were *Beloved* and *Making History*, your task might be:

'Explore the ways Friel uses settings of place **and** time for dramatic effect in *Making History*.

Then *either*:

'Compare the ways *Making History* and other plays you have read use settings of place **and** time.'

or

'Compare the ways Friel uses setting of place **and** time in *Making History* with Morrison in *Beloved*.'

(You might like to start with presentation of ideas about the relevance of history beyond living memory.)

■ If the two chosen texts were *The Handmaid's Tale* and *Top Girls*, your task might be:

'Explore the ways Churchill presents women in her play.'

Then *either*:

'Compare the ways *Top Girls* and other plays about the struggle for identity present women.'

or

'Compare the ways Churchill presents women with the ways Atwood presents the female characters in *The Handmaid's Tale*.'

■ If the two chosen texts were *Snow Falling on Cedars* and *Death and the King's Horseman*, your task might be:

'Explore the ways Soyinka presents ideas about duty and honour in his play.'

Then **either**:

'Compare the ways *Death and the King's Horseman* and other plays about the struggle for identity present ideas about duty and honour.'

or

'Compare the ways Soyinka presents ideas about duty and honour with the ways Guterson presents ideas about duty and honour in *Snow Falling on Cedars*.'

(You might like to start with the presentation of identities and actions of Elesin, the King's Horseman, and Ishmael Chambers.)

Activity

Write as many tasks as you can on the aspect of your chosen text that interests you. You can do this individually, with a partner, or in a group. You can then share your tasks with your partner or the group, and get your teacher to check that they are appropriate.

Summary

Success in your coursework will depend on:

- careful choice of texts
- the negotiation of two clearly focused tasks
- planning your time so as to make the best use of the opportunities offered by coursework
- developing a clear line of argument
- maintaining a focus on the writers' choices of form, structure and language
- developing the points you make and supporting them with close reference to the text and appropriate quotation
- your personal engagement with and independent thinking about your texts.

4   Tackling wider reading in poetry

💡 Introduction

This chapter and the two chapters that follow introduce you to ways of reading widely in the literature of 'The Struggle for Identity in Modern Literature' and prepare you for the context question of Unit 1, which is dealt with later in this book, in Chapter 7. This chapter focuses on **poetry**: the two chapters that follow deal with **prose** and **drama**.

Structure of the chapter

Before we turn our attention to the poetry itself, we will begin with some ideas about how modern readers might see poetry now.

Because the idea of 'The Struggle for Identity in Modern Literature' may seem to have a rather large and flexible context, this chapter will outline the **key contexts** – historical, social and political – that have influenced, in one way or another, all the literature you will encounter on your AS course as part of 'The Struggle for Identity in Modern Literature'. This outline is therefore equally relevant to Chapter 3 (coursework), the wider reading, Chapters 5 (prose) and 6 (drama), and Chapter 7 (non-fiction).

The background will help us to see the contexts in which modern poetry operates and assist our exploration and linking of poems.

This chapter is in five sections:

1   The current status of poetry
2   Some history to put the literature into context
3   The outcome
4   The conclusion for poetry
5   The poetry itself.

■ The current status of poetry

The fading genre

Poetry, it might appear, did become the late 20th century's least favourite, least popular and least read of all the literary genres, particularly among young adults. Had you chosen one of the other two options for study on this unit – World War One or The Victorians – and were now consulting the companion textbook for either of those, you would read this about poetry in their respective Chapter 4 introductions:

'Poetry is, as you will have realised, the dominant genre in World War One writing.'

'For the Victorians, poetry was the most elevated of literary art forms. In the nineteenth century, poets were often revered as moral educators whose role was to teach their readers the right ways to think and feel.'

Poetry in school

Yet A Level students represent a fair cross section of society when they claim that poetry makes their heads hurt. It was not always so. At nursery and primary school, creativity through verse is at a premium. You had lively recitals of poems for children, even universal 'adult' examples from Blake, like 'Tyger, Tyger …' (bet you can finish the line!) – and remember the precious efforts you perhaps made yourself for loved ones and family in classroom activities, producing cards for social and religious celebrations.

It does not stop there. A teacher of English literature may receive several heartfelt notebook outpourings from sixth-form students, confessing thoughts and feelings on their latest muse, lover, personal crisis, international disaster, state of the world, their own desperate condition, and so on. This is not to mock, not at all, but to come clean about the universal role that writing poetry, competing for your attention alongside music, drama, sport, friendship and conversation, can play in the crucial self-development of any student – anyone like you. How do you think the likes of Morrissey, Pete Doherty, 2pak Shakur and Missy Elliot started their careers as wordsmiths? Probably angst-ridden in their bedrooms or gazing out of the bus window; perhaps like you.

What's wrong with poetry?

So why is it that the most common complaint a teacher might hear about the study of poetry, even at this level, is, 'I don't get it'?

Why does poetry sadly remain the literature of those perceived as the largely unenvied intellectual elite? Privileged, wealthy, distant intellectuals; the literati; owl-glassed broadsheet readers. Poetry has gained the tags of impenetrable and irrelevant, and boring. But worse than this, out of date and old …

Even if you feel the muse move you and can accept these labels, if you are young you certainly will not want to be seen as an 'oldie'. Poetry is simply not sexy. And to use another ambiguity, it does not seem to come easy. It is this lack of fashion and lack of accessibility that has threatened our relationship individually and socially with this most powerful of literary forms. In competition with instantly gratifying models of the digital screen, like film, television, text and games, poetry after World War One fell out of favour in popular culture.

The purpose of this chapter

All we are saying is … give poetry a chance. See this genre for what it really is and can continue to be, for all of us, if we allow it to. In the modern literature that shows us many different struggles for identity, poetry has three bright torches to burn:

1 It gives us a ready form of self-expression through our own writing, when we need to come to terms with ourselves and our own feelings – **it provides for us a self-identity**.

2 Through our reading of others, when we realise 'I felt that' but could not say it – through lack of the words we wanted to use, even lack of recognition that we had felt it at all, for lack of support around us to say confidently who we are and what we want – **it provides for us a social identity**.

3 It teaches us about the lives and experiences of others with identities remote from our own; it broadens our horizons and gives us choices on how to think and feel, so that we become more than we were before we took the trouble to understand something beyond ourselves – **it educates us**.

Some history to put the literature into context

What the 20th century offers us is unique in the history and development of literature, in this case poetry. As the popularity and status of this establishment genre dwindled and collapsed, so did the dominant ideologies the world had previously accepted or fought. Probably for similar reasons, they had both had largely the same beneficiaries, the ruling class. Poetry was seen as refined, often catering for the supposed 'higher sensibilities' of the educated, leisure classes. The dominant pre-existing ideologies, as suggested below, were organised for the promotion of the rich and powerful, the only ones with much of this leisure time.

What changed?

The Victorian construct of empire and colonisation, its wealth built on slavery and distributed through strict social class and gender divisions and rules, was challenged throughout the 20th century, and in many cases defeated. This began with the changed societies growing initially out of World Wars One and Two.

The modern era

The modern era, and therefore its literature, shifted this belief to one that asked for a share of the power and wealth – democracy. With it came the leisure and freedom to pursue this new status, this new identity, the importance of the individual. Achieving a 'new identity' was not so easy. The 20th century was thus tumultuous in its events and extreme in its solutions.

Nowhere is this more visible than in its literature. Poetry became the ideal vehicle for expressing self-identity and – if easy to remember and recite, set to music or a beat – a rousing call to publicise social identity. The main differences between modern poetry and its ancestors are threefold:

1 Poetry, like power, wealth and the vote, was now to be for all people.
2 Poetry could adopt any form, any metre, any rhythm. The old rules, likes the chains of its creators, were there to be broken. Poetry needed new ways to express the freedom of participation that the modern era offered poets. **Free verse** was born.
3 Poetry of the **vernacular** developed: new poetic languages drew on sounds, words and structures which celebrated different varieties of English. There was a new focus on the speech patterns of people's regional accents and dialects. This was expressed by the 1960s Liverpool 'Merseybeat' poets, Roger McGough, Brian Patten and Adrian Henri, and in the USA by the 'beat generation' poets like Allen Ginsberg, whose collection *Howl* is on your wider reading list. Languages like Jamaican Creole, which had grown from a blend of English and African languages used by African slaves and their English owners to communicate in the Caribbean colonies, became a rich source to explore experiences that could not be fruitfully shared in Standard English. This can be seen, for example, in the poetry of Linton Kwesi Johnson.

Words and their power

The 20th century gave us the vocabulary of 'racism', 'sexism' and 'homophobia'. We gained a heightened awareness of the concepts of 'social class struggle', 'anarchy', 'national liberation' and 'apartheid'. The most unsettling idea is that of a literal unsettling, that of the 'refugee'; the 'immigrant', the 'migrant worker', the 'asylum seeker', the 'unwelcome invader'.

Refugee status

There is nothing at all new about this movement of people, particularly in Britain, whose history back to the Stone Age will show you. It is also how the modern, post-colonial societies of the USA and Australia were built. However, in 21st-century Britain it has taken on something of a sinister cloak. Some would argue this is simply economic. The post-war refugees and colonial immigrants to England, the USA and Australia between the 1940s and 1970s were deemed necessary to rebuild these economies and, quite literally, the countries. Now that is done, the people are seen as unnecessary and are believed to present a threat to culture and to be an economic burden. This is perhaps a matter of attitude rather than logical fact.

Racial purity

Without this long-established intermingling of races and people, England, with its Viking place names up the east coast and its French additions to the agricultural and linguistic developments of its past, would still be sharpening flints in the forest. The widespread realisation of a belief in 'racial purity and supremacy' was, of course, the philosophy of the National Socialist Party of the Third Reich, the Nazis.

This legacy influenced the far right-wing Nationalist movement from the 1930s in Britain, manifest in the National Front in the 1970s and now the British National Party, with its central ideology 'England for the English' and a narrow racial definition of what that constitutes. Their history has been tarnished with charges of racism, fascism and sectarian violence – all anathema to a democracy.

Similarly, the ethnic cleansing of the Balkans throughout the 1980s and 1990s is accepted as one of the atrocities of modern European history. The second rise of the political far right in Europe mirrors its 1930 origins: high unemployment and poverty linked to the propaganda that someone – for example an ethnic group – must be to blame rather than something systematic such as inevitable troughs in the capitalist economic cycle of boom and recession.

Solidarity

Of course, it is not the case that all the English were murderous and powerful landowners or embittered avengers, intent on suppressing women and promoting heterosexuality, exploiting the 'ordinary man', repelling the cultural invader and stealing their countries from under them. Apart from those who 'turned native', to the puzzlement of their superiors, there were many who joined the ranks in various struggles, whether or not they had any personal gain to make from a victorious outcome for the 'underdog'. From this, we have the idea of 'solidarity', expressed in the 1970s Chilean slogan 'El pueblo unido jamás será vencido' (The people united will never be defeated), and sung by protest movements all over the world today.

■ The outcome

However, despite a promising 20th-century start to overcoming the struggles for identity and expressing and achieving the fulfilled self and social group, the world does not seem to have come very far in the first decade of the 21st century. It has even been argued that some sections of society seem somewhat gripped in a backlash against civil, even human, rights, and against society's most vulnerable members.

The 21 century will reveal whether the global capitalist system allows all people, whatever their race, gender, social class and culture, to function and flourish equally. You can experience and participate as events unfold and decide for yourself. The modern literature of 'struggles for identity' will no doubt continue to document and explore the individual and social responses to concepts of equality and self-determination and experiences of injustice. You, in turn, can read or even write them.

The role of language

Paradoxically, the wealth of international literature written in English exists only because of the former British Empire and its colonisation. Britain, like the other European seafaring superpowers, in particular Spain, Portugal, Holland and France, exported its culture, religion and, most importantly, its language, across the globe. The policy of 'Anglicisation' contributed to successful foreign rule. Take away a people's language, customs and belief system and you have them subdued and unable to forge a common identity, as a group or individually. The less successful and much older colonisations, which still are unresigned to the annexation of their countries, notably England's Gaelic and Celtic neighbours – Ireland, Scotland and Wales – interestingly see the restoration of the mother language as part of reclaiming a national identity. This policy has been most successful in Wales, with many schools educating children through the Welsh language.

Of course, social disintegration and poverty, inequality and the loss of spoken languages, happen in England, as the literature shows, through the disenfranchisement of the ordinary people whom the welfare state, liberation movements and social class struggles have worked so hard to empower.

■ The conclusion for poetry

We are left with the gift of a double-edged sword – the literary expression of identities offered for study in this unit have come out of struggle which, by its nature, implies **suffering** – of the self or the society from which the literature came. It remains uplifting when we come across an example of **resistance** literature, and an inspiration when we encounter the literature of **renewal and self-determination**.

We are now going to look in detail at some poetry that reflects these issues and demonstrates different struggles for identity in modern literature.

We will adopt a thematic approach with two perspectives, the 'self' and the 'social' and, in turn, consider:

- poetry of suffering
- poetry of resistance
- poetry of renewal and self-determination.

You need to keep a record of your discoveries so that you develop a reading diary – this may be in a file on paper or by using the **e-resource.**

🔍 The poetry itself

The poetry of suffering

The 'self'

It is dangerous to generalise and difficult to categorise the meaning and differences of 'self' and 'social'. However, broadly speaking, we can identify poetry concerned with the idea of the 'self' as being inward-looking, possibly, but not always, told by or about a single individual, and relating an experience that is personally felt rather than identifying with the experiences of others. Of course, that does not mean it cannot be felt by others, but it tends to convey feelings perhaps experienced in isolation and separated from a common human bond.

We are going to look at a poem from *The Dead Sea Poems* by Simon Armitage, a Yorkshire man born in 1963, and published in 1995 by Faber and Faber. This collection contains many poems which wrestle with the role of the self in this society. They range in mood and outcome, but all attempt to explore the response of individuals when 'identity' is under question or threat. Here, as an example of the poetry of suffering, we are presented with a persona who suffers alienation – alone, rejected and desperate, with no ability to struggle or carve a sense of identity for him or herself.

Extract A

Give

Of all the public places, dear
To make a scene, I've chosen here.

Of all the doorways in the world
To choose to sleep, I've chosen yours.
I'm on the street, under the stars.

For coppers I can dance or sing.
For silver – swallow swords, eat fire.
For gold – escape from locks and chains.

It's not as if I'm holding out
For frankincense or myrrh, just change.

You give me tea. That's big of you.
I'm on my knees. I beg of you.

Simon Armitage

Fig. 4.1 *A young homeless person begging in a city street doorway*

■ Questions

AO1: Developing an informed response to the text

■ What thoughts and feelings does Armitage express in this poem?

AO2: Understanding how structure, form and language shape meaning

■ Explore the language which Armitage uses to express his thoughts and feelings.

■ What is the impact of using direct address, 'yours' in verse two and repetition of 'you' in the last verse?

■ Comment on the effect and uses of metaphor and allusion in verse four, in particular, the words 'frankincense or myrrh, just change'.

■ Consider the effect of using full stops midline in the final verse.

■ **AO3: Exploring connections, comparisons and the interpretations of other readers**

■ Consider the significance of this poem in relation to the title of the collection, *The Dead Sea Poems*.

■ Compare this poem with others from the collection and trace any connections in ideas, themes and subject matter.

■ Explore any similarities and differences you discover between this poem and other poems concerned with a focus on 'the self'.

■ Compare this poem with 'Afterword', the Nichols poem later in this chapter, and make a note of the differences you find.

■ A critic has said that 'this poem represents the poetry of self-pity and tries to make the reader feel responsible for the suffering of the beggar who could clearly help himself instead of sponging off others. Armitage is irresponsible for endorsing lazy dependence on charity in his portrayal of this weak and sorry soul.'
How do you respond to this interpretation of Armitage's 'Give'?

AO4: Understanding the significance and influence of contexts

■ How does this poem reflect the context of the poetry of suffering in the struggle for identity? Consider both subject matter and style.

Make sure you keep your notes on this poem and its connections in your Reading Log.

The 'social'

Poetry concerned with a 'social' focus tends to deal with the experiences of groups rather than individuals. Such poetry may draw connections across that group to highlight, in the case of the poetry of suffering, issues of common persecution or marginalisation.

This poem, 'Refugee Blues', was written by W.H. Auden in 1939 and can be found in *W.H. Auden Poems* selected by John Fuller, published by Faber and Faber in 2000. It focuses on the life-threatening plight of German Jewish people after Hitler and the Nazis seized power in Germany in 1930. At this time, many Jews saw the dreadful signs around them of what was to come, and tried, unsuccessfully, to leave their homes and country.

W.H. Auden (1907–1973) was a young man when he heard of these events and wrote this poem. Neither German nor Jewish – in fact English, white and upper-middle-class, his poetry often deals with larger social and political concerns. Often, as here, he writes about how he sees the injustices of his time. He presents a different type of homelessness and loss of identity to the previous Armitage poem.

■ Further reading

The Big Issue (magazine supporting homeless people)

The Child in Time, Ian McEwan (1980s novel on Thatcher years in Britain)

'The Good Samaritan' (biblical fable)

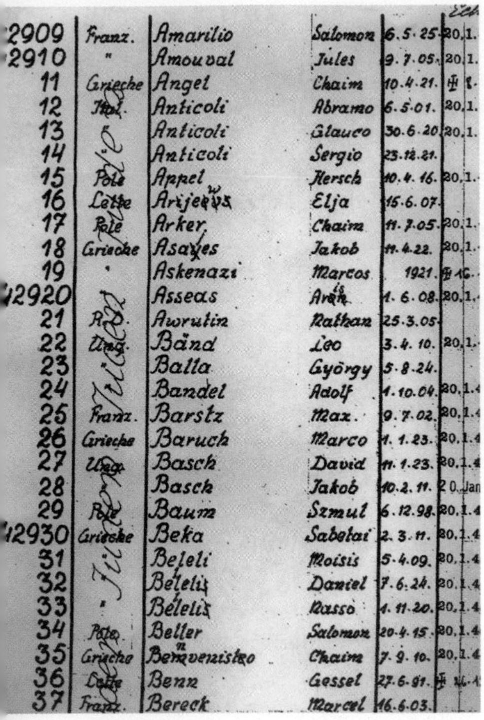

2909	Franz.	Amarilio	Salomon	6.5.25	20.1.
2910	"	Amouval	Jules	9.7.05	20.1.
11	Grieche	Angel	Chaim	10.4.21	
12	Ital.	Anticoli	Abramo	6.5.01	20.1.
13		Anticoli	Glauco	30.6.20	20.1.
14		Anticoli	Sergio	23.12.21	
15	Pole	Appel	Hersch	10.4.16	20.1.
16	Lette	Arijeews	Elja	15.6.07	
17	Pole	Arker	Chaim	11.7.05	20.1.
18	Grieche	Asayes	Jakob	11.4.22	20.1.
19	"	Askenazi	Marcos	1921	
12920		Asseas	Aron	1.6.08	20.1.
21	R.	Awrutin	Nathan	25.3.05	
22	Ung.	Bänd	Leo	3.4.10	20.1.
23		Balla	György	5.8.24	
24		Bandel	Adolf	1.10.04	20.1.4
25	Franz.	Barstz	Max	9.7.02	20.1.4
26	Grieche	Baruch	Marco	1.1.23	20.1.4
27	Ung.	Basch	David	11.1.23	20.1.4
28		Basch	Jakob	10.2.11	20.Jan
29	Pole	Baum	Szmul	6.12.98	20.1.4
12930	Grieche	Beka	Sabetai	2.3.11	20.1.4
31		Beleli	Moisis	5.4.09	20.1.4
32		Beleli	Daniel	7.6.24	20.1.4
33	"	Beleli	Rasso	1.11.20	20.1.4
34	Pole	Beller	Salomon	20.4.15	20.1.4
35	Grieche	Benvenisto	Chaim	7.9.10	20.1.4
36	Lette	Benn	Gessel	27.6.91	
37	Franz.	Bereck	Marcel	16.6.03	

Fig. 4.2 *A list of the Jews incarcerated by the Nazis in the Echterdingen World War Two forced labour camp, taken from a list of camp inmates*

Further reading

Anne Frank, *Diary of a Young Girl* (autobiography from Holland, in hiding, translated from the Dutch)

Thomas Keneally, *Schindler's Ark* (Australian novel written in the 1980s)

Primo Levi, *If this is a man* (autobiography from Auschwitz, translated from the Italian)

Pastor Niemoller, 'First they came for…' (poem from World War Two on Nazi concentration camps)

Extract B

Refugee Blues

Say this city has ten million souls
Some are living in mansions, some are living in holes:
Yet there's no place for us, my dear, yet there's no place for us.

Once we had a country and we thought it fair,
Look in the atlas and you'll find it there:
We cannot go there now, my dear, we cannot go there now.

In the village churchyard there grows an old yew,
Every Spring it blossoms anew:
Old passports can't do that, my dear, old passports can't do that.

The consul banged the table and said:
'If you've got no passport you're officially dead';
But we are still alive, my dear, but we are still alive.

Went to a committee: they offered me a chair;
Asked me politely to return next year:
But where shall we go today, my dear, but where shall we go today?

Came to a public meeting, the speaker got up and said:
'If we let them in, they will steal our daily bread';
He was talking of you and me, my dear, he was talking of you and me.

Thought I heard the thundering rumbling in the sky;
It was Hitler over Europe, saying: 'They must die';
O we were in his mind, my dear, O we were in his mind.

Saw a poodle in a jacket fastened with a pin,
Saw a door opened and a cat let in:
But they weren't German Jews, my dear, but they weren't German Jews.

Went down the harbour and stood upon the quay,
Saw the fish swimming as if they were free:
Only ten feet away, my dear, only ten feet away.

Walked through a wood, saw the birds in the trees;
They had no politicians and sang at their ease:
They weren't the human race, my dear, they weren't the human race.

Dreamed I saw a building with a thousand floors,
A thousand windows and a thousand doors;
Not one of them was ours, my dear, not one of them was ours.

Stood on a great plain in the falling snow;
Ten thousand soldiers marched to and fro:
Looking for you and me, my dear, looking for you and me.

W.H. Auden

■ Questions

AO1: Developing an informed response to the text

■ Describe what is happening in this poem.

■ What thoughts and feelings are presented to the reader?

AO2: Understanding how structure, form and language shape meaning

■ What do you notice about the language Auden has chosen to describe the events and present these thoughts and feelings?

■ How does Auden use rhyme, repetition and rhetorical questions to shape meaning?

■ Explore the use and effect of natural imagery in the poem.

■ AO3: Exploring connections, comparisons and the interpretations of other readers

■ Compare this poem with others from the selection, for example: 'O What is That Sound' (1932), and sometimes entitled 'The Quarry'; 'Spain 1937' (1937); 'Here war is simple like a monument' (1938); 'Musée des Beaux Arts' (1938).

■ What links can you find with other poems you have read which express a 'social' identity?

■ Compare this poem with Extract D 'The School Among the Ruins' in the next section, **The poetry of resistance**.

■ How do you respond to the view that this poem has a childish rhythm, an awkward rhyme and an unconvincing tone?

■ John Fuller has said, in the Introduction to the selection, that Auden's poetic aim was to 'express the thoughts of a wise man in the language of the common people'. How far do you think Auden has achieved this in 'Refugee Blues'?

AO4: Understanding the significance and influence of contexts

■ What do you find interesting about the title 'Refugee Blues'? What do you feel is the relevance for us now of the poem's ideas and subject matter?

■ How typical do you find this as an example of modern anti-war poetry?

■ Auden was heavily criticised for leaving Britain for America during World War Two. There was a belief that he abandoned the suffering of the people to escape the war. How do you respond to this idea after reading the poem?

■ How does this poem reflect the events at the time of writing?

The poetry of resistance

The 'self'

This poem, 'Hell is Round the Corner', is taken from *The Fire People: A Collection of Contemporary Black British Poets*, edited by Lemn Sissay and published in 1998 by Payback Press. It is written by Tricky, a Bristol-born rapper, and became the lyrics to the song of the same name on his 1995 album *Maxinquaye*.

Like the previous Armitage poem focused on the idea of 'the self', this poem is concerned with the experiences and feelings of alienation of a single persona, is written in the first person and addressed to an unknown 'you'. The viewpoint of the outcast is again clear, but this time appears to stem from the experience of racism narrated by the persona in the poem.

However, as an example of the poetry of resistance, this poem explores the notion of fighting back and maintaining the struggle for identity. The persona criticises the source of this struggle, challenging stereotypes imposed on the subject of the poem. In contrast to 'Give' (Extract A), whatever 'hell' is experienced, she or he does not appear to succumb to a subservient role, despite the alienation documented in the poem.

Fig. 4.3 *Tricky performs*

Extract C

Hell is Round the Corner

I stand firm for a soil, I lick a rock off foil
Reduce me, seduce me, dress me up in Stussy
Hell is round the corner where I shelter,
Isms and schisms, we're living on a skelter
If you believe I'll deceive and common sense says you are the thief
Let me take you down the corridors of my life.

And when you walk do you walk to your preference
No need to answer till I take further evidence
I seem to need a reference to get residence
A reference to your preference to say
I'm a good neighbour
I trudge, so judge me for my labour
Lobotomy ensures my good behaviour

A constant struggle ensures my insanity
Passive indifference ensures
The struggle for my family
We're hungry beware of our appetite
Distant drums bring the news of a kill tonight
The kill which I share with my passengers
We take our fill take our fill take a feel.

Confused by different memories, details of Asian remedies
Conversations of what's become of enemies
My brain thinks bomb-like, so I listen he's a con kike
(And as I grow) As I grow, I grow collective
Before the move sit on the perspective
Mr Quail's in the crevice and watches from the precipice
Imperial passage
Heat from the sun someday slowly passes
Until then, you have to live with yourself
Until then, you have to live with yourself

I stand firm for a soil, I lick a rock off foil
Reduce me, seduce me, dress me up in Stussy
Hell is round the corner where I shelter,
Isms and schisms, we're living on a skelter
If you believe I'll deceive and common sense says you are the thief
Let me take you down the corridors of my life.

My brain thinks bomb-like; bomb-like
Beware of our appetite.

Tricky also known as Adam Thaws

Questions

AO1: Developing an informed response to the text

■ What events and experiences are described in the poem?

■ What thoughts and feelings are expressed?

AO2: Understanding how structure, form and language shape meaning

■ This poem is set to music. Explore how rhyme, rhythm and repetition are used to deliver the words and ideas in a spoken format.

■ Explore the effects of Tricky's use of vocabulary.

AO3: Exploring connections, comparisons and the interpretations of other readers

■ Compare this poem with others from the collection, for example: 'On finally wiping the swastika from the bus stop', 'Colour Blind' and 'Gift'.

■ What connections can you make between this poem and other poems by black writers you have read?

■ Compare this poem to other examples of 'resistance poetry' you have read.

■ What differences and what similarities have you noticed in terms of subject matter and style?

■ How do you respond to the view that the violence suggested by the persona will only increase the alienation he or she feels within the hostile society?

AO4: Understanding the significance and influence of contexts

■ How does this poem reflect the urban struggle for cultural and racial acceptance?

■ How does this poem present stereotypes applied to black African and Caribbean people?

Further reading

Listen to *Maxinquaye* by Tricky

Lemn Sissay, *Morning Breaks in the Elevator*

Benjamin Zephaniah, *Too Black Too Strong*

The poetry of Langston Hughes

The poetry of Bobby Sands, from *Skylark Sing Your Lonely Song*

The 'social'

The following poem is the title poem from *The School Among the Ruins* by the American poet Adrienne Rich, published by Norton in 2005. Like Auden, Rich is famously a champion for the persecuted. She has publicly condemned the war on terror and this poem is a graphic documentary of that condemnation.

Extract D

The School Among the Ruins
Beirut.Baghdad.Sarajevo.Bethlehem.Kabul. Not of course here.

1
Teaching the first lesson and the last
– great falling light of summer will you last
longer than schooltime?
When children flow
in columns at the doors
BOYS GIRLS and the busy teachers

open or close high windows
with hooked poles drawing darkgreen shades

closets unlocked, locked
questions unasked, asked, when

love of the fresh impeccable
sharp-pencilled   yes
order without cruelty

a street on earth   neither heaven nor hell
busy with commerce and worship
young teachers walking to school

fresh bread and early-open foodstalls

2
When the offensive rocks the sky when nightglare
misconstrues day and night when lived-in
rooms from the upper city
tumble cratering lower streets

cornices of olden ornament   human debris
when fear vacuums out the streets

When the whole town flinches
blood on the undersole thickening to glass

Whoever crosses   hunched   knees bent   a contested
zone
knows why she does this suicidal thing

School's now in session day and night
children sleep
in the classrooms   teachers rolled close

3
How the good teacher loved
his school the students
the lunchroom with fresh sandwiches

lemonade and milk
the classroom glass cages
of moss and turtles
teaching responsibility

A morning breaks without bread or fresh-poured milk
parents or lesson plans

diarrhea first question of the day
children shivering it's September
Second question: where is my mother?

4
One: I don't know where your mother
is Two: I don't know
why they are trying to hurt us
Three: or the latitude and longitude
of their hatred Four: I don't know if we
hate them as much   I think there's more toilet paper
in the supply closet   I'm going to break it open

Today this is your lesson:
write as clearly as you can
your name   home street   and number
down on this page
No you can't go home yet
but you aren't lost
this is our school

I'm not sure what we'll eat
we'll look for healthy roots and greens
searching for water though the pipes are broken

5
There's a young cat sticking
her head through window bars
she's hungry like us
but can feed on mice
her bronze erupting fur
speaks of a life already wild

her golden eyes
don't give quarter   She'll teach us   Let's call her
Sister
when we get milk we'll give her some

6
I've told you, let's try to sleep in this funny camp
All night pitiless pilotless things go shrieking
above us to somewhere

Don't let your faces turn to stone
Don't stop asking me why
Let's pay attention to our cat   she needs us

Maybe tomorrow the bakers can fix their ovens

7
'We sang them to naps told stories made
shadow animals with our hands

wiped human debris off boots and coats
sat learning by heart the names
some were too young to write
some had forgotten how'

Adrienne Rich, 2001

■ Questions

AO1: Developing an informed response to the text

■ Explore what is happening in the poem.

■ Explore the significance of its subtitle, particularly the phrase 'Not of course here'.

■ What thoughts and feelings do the speakers express?

AO2: Understanding how structure, form and language shape meaning

■ How does the poet's choice of language help to present her thoughts and feelings?

■ Explore the ways she uses form and structure within and across each section of the poem.

AO3: Exploring connections, comparisons and the interpretations of other readers

■ What connections can you make with other examples of resistance poetry you have read?

■ What connections can you make with other examples of poems about social issues?

■ Compare this poem with: Rich's 'Wait' and 'Transparencies' from the same collection; other modern anti-war poems, for example Tony Harrison's 'A Cold Coming' and Carol Ann Duffy's 'Loud from Feminine Gospels'; other poems about a school day, like Carol Ann Duffy's 'In Mrs Tilcher's Class'. What differences and similarities do you notice?

■ How do you respond to the view that the poem is too much like propaganda to be effective poetry?

AO4: Understanding the significance and influence of context

■ Explore how this poem uses the combined universal contexts of war and childhood to communicate the specific context of a very particular time and place.

■ Further reading

A Cold Coming: Gulf War Poems, Tony Harrison (1990), published by Bloodaxe Books

Mezzaterra, Fragments from the Common Ground (Section 1 'Political Essays', some on the Israeli-Palestinian War), Ahdaf Soueif (2004), published by Bloomsbury (from your non-fiction wider reading list)

'Now I'll Kill You!', Eileen Brennan – Crossmaglen (1998), from *Women's Stories from the North of Ireland*, edited by Silvia Calamati, 2002, published by Beyond the Pale (autobiographical interviews from your non-fiction wider reading list)

Fig. 4.4 *Group of schoolchildren in the Balkans*

The poetry of renewal and self-determination

The self

In the poetry of renewal and self-determination, we see a departure in expressions of identity of the 'self'. Self-identity here has reached its goal: to exist as a right, a human right simply to be, whatever your background, circumstances, experiences and choices. Maya Angelou said on the subject of self-identity that the art is not to survive but to thrive; to celebrate who you are as an individual and refuse to be contained or destroyed. The goal is self-acceptance, whether social acceptance has been achieved or not. The 'self' in this state of self-awareness and equal status is fulfilled, but, like the rest of humanity, not necessarily happy with an easy life.

This poem, 'Funeral Blues', is by W.H. Auden, whose work 'Refugee Blues', you encountered earlier in the chapter. While the title and time of composition may appear to be similar, this poem explores a very different identity of self-determination and the right 'to be', in contrast with the previous poem which focused on social suffering. Here Auden's sexuality as a gay man is made clear through the speaker's gender-specific public tribute to and grief for his dead love.

You might be wondering how this poem and its subject matter could represent renewal and self-determination as it is about death and loss. This poem was published 30 years before it was legal in Britain even to *be* gay. Gay sexual relationships were punished by imprisonment under the Sexual Offences Act until 1967, making it a crime to express consenting sexual love between adults of the same sex. You can only admire Auden's stance that whatever the cost to his reputation, privacy and security, he will celebrate and grieve his love. Despite its subject matter, it is a triumph of liberated self-identity.

Extract E

> **Funeral Blues**
>
> Stop all the clocks, cut off the telephone,
> Prevent the dog from barking with a juicy bone,
> Silence the pianos and with muffled drum
> Bring out the coffin, let the mourners come.
>
> Let aeroplanes circle moaning overhead
> Scribbling on the sky the message He Is Dead,
> Put crepe bows round the white necks of the public doves,
> Let the traffic policemen wear black cotton gloves.
>
> He was my North, my South, my East and West,
> My working week and my Sunday rest,
> My noon, my midnight, my talk, my song;
> I thought that love would last forever: I was wrong.
>
> The stars are not wanted now; put out every one,
> Pack up the moon and dismantle the sun,
> Pour away the ocean and sweep up the wood;
> For nothing now can ever come to any good.
>
> *W.H. Auden, 1936*

■ Questions

AO1: Developing an informed response to the text

■ What are the thoughts and feelings expressed in the poem?

💡 AO2: Understanding how structure, form and language shape meaning

■ How do Auden's choices of language and structure enable him to express those thoughts and feelings?

AO3: Exploring connections, comparisons and the interpretations of other readers

■ What connections can you make between this poem and other poems you have read on the subject and idea of self-determination and renewal?

■ What connections can you make between this poem and other poems which express the struggle for identity of the 'self'?

■ Compare this poem with other Auden love poems, for example, 'O Tell Me the Truth about Love', 'Lullabye', 'The More Loving One', 'As I Walked Out One Evening', and 'Lay your sleeping head, my love'.

■ Compare the poem with Carol Ann Duffy's poem 'White Writing' from *Feminine Gospels* (2002), about celebrating love without the possibility of marriage.

■ Compare the poem with Douglas Dunn's poem, 'Reincarnations from Elegies' (1985), lyric love poetry written about the death of his wife.

■ What similarities and differences do you notice across these poems?

■ How do you respond to the claim that in this poem 'Auden is being ironic not passionate'?

AO4: Understanding the significance and influence of contexts

■ How does this poem reflect its early 20th-century context?

■ How does it transcend its time of writing?

■ Further reading

As detailed opposite under AO3

Allen Ginsberg, *Howl* (1956)

Langston Hughes

Audre Lorde, 1970–1990s

Gertrude Stein, *Tender Buttons* (1920)

Alice Walker, *Revolutionary Petunias* (1970)

The 'social'

The poem 'Afterword' (overleaf) was written by Grace Nichols as part of a collection called *The Fat Black Woman's Poems*, published by Virago in 1984. It focuses on the situation and status of black women, fat or otherwise, in Western thought and society.

Grace Nichols (1950–) is a black woman, but not noticeably fat – much as Auden was not Jewish and Rich was not from the Middle East. Like Auden and Rich, Nichols is often concerned with larger social and political concerns and their impact on oppressed people, particularly black women. Born in Guyana, she has lived in England since 1977.

Extract F

Afterword

The fat black woman
will come out of the forest
brushing vegetations
from the shorn of her hair

flaunting waterpearls
in the bush of her thighs
blushing wet in the morning
sunlight

the fat black woman will sigh
there will be an immense joy
in the full of her eye
as she beholds

behold now the fat black woman
who will come out of the forest

when the last of her race
is finally and utterly extinguished

when the wind pushes back the last curtain
of male white blindness

the fat black woman will emerge
and tremblingly fearlessly

stake her claim again

Grace Nichols

Fig. 4.5 *'The fat black woman will come out of the forest. . .'*

■ Questions

AO1: Developing an informed response to the text

■ What are the thoughts and feelings expressed in the poem?

■ What is the significance of the title of the poem?

AO2: Understanding how structure, form and language shape meaning

■ How do Nichols' choices of language and structure enable her to express those thoughts and feelings?

■ How does the setting help to create meaning in the poem?

AO3: Exploring connections, comparisons and the interpretations of other readers

■ What connections can you make between this poem and others you have read with the subject matter and idea of self-determination and renewal?

■ What connections can you make between this poem and those you have read that express a struggle for 'social' identity?

■ Compare this poem with other poems from the collection, for example, 'Beauty', 'The Assertion', 'Invitation' and 'Holding my Beads'; Alice Walker's poem 'The Nature of This Flower is To Bloom' from *Revolutionary Petunias and other poems* (1970); Maya Angelou's poem 'Still I Rise' from *And Still I Rise* (1978). What similarities and differences do you notice?

■ How do you respond to the claim that in this poem 'Nichols creates a persona who rejoices in herself'?

AO4: Understanding the significance and influence of contexts

■ How does this poem reflect its late 20th-century context?

■ How typical do you think this poem is of poetry you have read by other black women?

■ Further reading

As detailed in AO3 opposite

'The Gift' by Labi Siffre from *The Fire People: A Collection of Contemporary Black British Poets* (1998)

Life Mask, Jackie Kay (2005)

The World's Wife, Carol Ann Duffy (1999)

The role of language in the modern poetry of self-determination

This chapter would not be complete without a look at **the role of language in the modern poetry of self-determination**. We looked earlier at expression of both the self and social identity through the poetic use of different varieties of English and integration of features from other languages from countries which Britain (England) had colonised.

There is a wealth of literature from most poets mentioned already, and several more, but we offer you one example, 'Fetch on the first of January' by the Scottish poet Liz Lochhead, from the collection *Dreaming Frankenstein* (1984). Lochhead was born in 1947 in Lanarkshire and her poetry has much to tell us about the experience of being female and growing older, and in particular about the role of language, the mother tongue, in self and social development.

This poem documents the Scottish tradition of first footing at the New Year, with the humorous slant of resisting unwelcome amorous advances and reminiscing with an old friend.

Extract G

Fetch on the first of January

Nae time eftir the Bells, and the
New Year new in wi' the
usual crowd, wi' whisky, cheers and kisses –
Ah'd aboot managed the windaes shut
some clown had thrown wide
hopin' tae hear the hooters on the Clyde
when the door went.
                Well, well,
who'd've thought Ah'd be staunin' there
tae first foot masel'?

This some kinnuffa Huntigowk for Hogmany?
Hell-mend-ye, ye're
a bad penny, Jimmy-
Mister Ne'erdy Ne'er-do-Weel
sae chitterin' ill-clad for the caul'
sae drawn an' pale,
oh, wi' the black bunburnin' a hole
in yir poackit an' the coal
a Live Coal.

'Gawn, get – Ah should shout it,
should shake a stick or ma fist,
oh but Ah should hunt ye, by Christ,
they wey you chased that big black tyke
that dogged ye wance, mind? –
a' the wey fae Hope Street hame.

Ah'll no let ye near me,
don't make me laugh,
got a much better
Better Half.
Och, aye tae glower at each other
was tae keek in a grey distortin' mirror
yet ye've the neck to come back again
wi yir bare face, Jake Fetch,
the image o' my ain.
Ice room yir mooth when ye kiss me
The cauld plumes o' yir breath
Ah'm lukkin daggers
You're lukkin like Death.
Ah'm damned if ye'll get past ma door,
nae fear!

Come away in, stranger, Happy New Year.

_____
Liz Lochhead

Questions

AO1: Developing an informed response to the text
- What are the thoughts and feelings expressed in the poem?
- What is the significance of the last line of the poem?

AO2: Understanding how structure, form and language shape meaning
- How do Lochhead's choices of language and structure enable her to express those thoughts and feelings?
- What is the effect of using Standard English in the last line?

AO3: Exploring connections, comparisons and the interpretations of other readers
- Compare this poem with other poems from the collection, for example, 'The Beltane Bride', 'Something I'm not', 'Poem on a Day Trip'; Jackie Kay's 'I kin see richt thru My Mither' from *Life Mask*, published in 2005; Tom Leonard's 'This is the Six o'Clock News' from *Intimate Exchanges*, published in 1984. What similarities and what differences do you notice?
- How do you respond to the criticism that in this poem Lochhead creates an impenetrable read with outmoded ideas?

AO4: Understanding the significance and influence of contexts
- How does this poem reflect a desire for self-determination through language?
- How does the poem highlight 'belonging' as a late 20th-century social concern?

Further reading

'I Neva Shot De Sherrif' from *Too Black, Too Strong* by Benjamin Zephaniah (2000)

Letters from a Far Country by Gillian Clarke (1985)

'On an Owd Piktcha' from *The Dead Sea Poems* by Simon Armitage (1995)

'Reggae fi May Ayim' by Linton Kwesi Johnson, from *The Fire People: A Collection of Contemporary Black British Poets* (1998)

Trainspotting, a novel by Irvine Welsh (1993)

'Translating the English', 'The Way my Mother Speaks', and 'Originally' from *The Other Country* by Carol Ann Duffy (1990)

Summary

- In this chapter we have looked at poetry that explores the struggle for identity in modern literature from the 1930s to the present day. The experiences of personal and social oppression and liberation contributed to the breadth of poetry which grew from radical 20th-century events and beliefs. This promoted for poets the possibilities of broader ideas and subject matter, wider use of language and language varieties, and changes in poetic form and structure. Since the collapse of empire and the wars and political conflicts of the last century, poets have claimed the right to express their varied concerns without the need for approval from the literary establishment.

- This idea of challenging the status quo through poetry is summed up in the Lochhead poem from 2003, 'Kidspoem/Bairnsang', in which she celebrates self and social identity through spoken and written language, and pins down the obstacles to free expression and self-determination in the following lines:

  Oh saying it was one thing
  but when it came to writing it
  in black and white
  the way it had to be said
  was as if you were posh, grown-up, male, English and dead.

  This chapter shows that modern poetry has perhaps outgrown that idea.

Tackling wider reading in prose

Introduction

In 'The Struggle for Identity in Modern Literature', the novel is harder to classify than the poetry of the previous chapter. The viewpoints taken by writers to explore perspectives of 'self' and 'social' identity are still useful to a study of prose. However, the ideas of 'suffering', 'resistance' and 'renewal and self-determination' also offered in Chapter 4 to consider poetry, are harder to embrace here. Therefore we need to consider the prose genre in a different way.

Structure of the chapter

This chapter will:

1 introduce the study of narrative viewpoint
2 outline basic features of prose fiction
3 provide wider reading novel extracts and activities for you to explore through a range of narrative viewpoints.

Narrative viewpoint

This chapter focuses on the writers' use of form. After all, the characters, whether real or imagined, only exist for us because the writer created them that way. We need to consider particular questions:

■ Through whose eyes and to what effect do we experience this tale?
■ Whose tale is it?
■ What kind of tale do they tell us?

We are going to consider novels with the following four narrative viewpoints:

■ The coming of age
■ The immigrant outsider
■ The local outsider
■ Identity in crisis: leaving the mainstream.

Before we do, it would be useful to consider some background to help you in your wider prose reading.

Basic features of prose fiction

Making meaning from modern novels

The genre of the novel is a **narrative**, a story told about **characters** and their journeys across a **setting** of a single or several places, real, imaginary or fantastic. A character may not achieve fulfilled self-development, but he or she will be presented as experiencing some change. Otherwise, the character will be static.

Without the characters and their journeys there will be no **plot**, no story told.

Narrative structure

Perhaps a novel will cover the range of ideas and experiences from 'suffering' through 'resistance' to 'renewal and self-determination', and this could be the 'self' or 'social' development presented through a central character. This could be told **chronologically**, moving forward through time and space, or in **flashback**, looking back in time and space from the past to the present.

Perhaps this character development will occur in an alternative **linear order**. Use of time may be represented in the narrative **simultaneously** across different characters, each one offering a single or changing grasp of their struggles. This is part of a **non-chronological** narrative style called a **split narrative**.

Alternatively, the story could move between realities, fantasies, dreams and even characters, with little emphasis on the notion of time to create separate but linked stories. They will all ultimately come together as part of the purpose of the novel, and maybe even chronologically by the novel's end, but they may be told separately during the progression of the narrative. You can also refer to this type of structure as a **split narrative**.

What is new: 'by the people for the people'

The new novelists are different from many of the Victorian moral educators, who were sometimes perhaps only observers of their subject matter. The modern era of fiction often presents the world from a position of personal experience and brings the marginalised voice to the foreground, rather than being expressed by someone else.

Link

For some historical context to set the scene for modern prose, see pp41–43.

Wider reading novel extracts

Now we turn to the wider reading novel extracts and activities for you to explore as examples of the four narrative viewpoints outlined earlier.

The coming of age

In these novels, the hero, heroine or central character grows up and leaves home. The home may have been literal or metaphorical, and the leaving, in turn, could be actual or developmental, emotionally and intellectually. The focus of the development is likely to be that of the 'self', even if social development is part of that. The hero/heroine may experience 'suffering' and may reach 'self-determination', but the genre is characterised by change and usually some 'self-realisation'. It is possible that by the end of the novel some reconciliation will take place towards the source/s of the conflict, and even a revisit to the scenes of the strife once the emergent identity of the hero/heroine is secure. The subject matter may be autobiographical, particularly based around childhood experiences and their impact on the adult 'self'. Family life and social hierarchies may be explored, for example the roles of parents, education, gender, class, nationality and sexuality. Sometimes these are set against bigger social backdrops such as war. Any narrative structure may be employed to convey the ideas of 'coming of age' novels.

This extract is taken from *Oranges Are Not the Only Fruit* by Jeanette Winterson (1985). This edition was published in 2001 by Vintage.

Here, towards the end of the novel, the heroine, Jeanette, must deal with the consequences of her mother's and the church's attitudes and decisions about her second sexual relationship with another young woman. In turn, her mother and the church must deal with the attitudes and decisions of the heroine.

Extract A

Pages 131–4, from the penultimate section, Judges

The days lingered on in a kind of numbness, me in ecclesiastical quarantine, then in a state of fear and anticipation. By Sunday the pastor had got word back from the council. The real problem, it seemed, was going against the teachings of St Paul, and allowing women power in the church. Our branch of the church had never thought about it, we'd always had strong women, and the women organised everything. Some of us could preach, and quite plainly, in my case, the church was full because of it. There was uproar, then a curious thing happened. My mother stood up and said she believed this was right: that women had specific circumstances for their ministry, that the Sunday school was one of them, the Sisterhood another, but the message belonged to the men. Until this moment my life had still made some kind of sense. Now it was making no sense at all. My mother droned on about the importance of missionary work for a woman, that I was clearly such a woman, but had spurned my call in order to wield power on the home front, where it was inappropriate. She ended by saying that having taken on a man's world in other ways I had flouted God's law and tried to do it sexually. This was no spontaneous speech. She and the pastor had talked about it already. It was her weakness for the ministry that had done it. No doubt she'd told Pastor Spratt months ago. I looked around me. Good people, simple people, what would happen to them now? I knew my mother hoped I would blame myself, but I didn't. I knew now where the blame lay. If there's such a thing as spiritual adultery, my mother was a whore.

…

Fig. 5.1 *Northern mill town*

Sir Perceval has been in the wood for many days now. His armour is dull, his horse tired. The last food he ate was a bowl of bread and milk given to him by an old woman. Other knights have been this way, he can see their tracks, their despair, for one, even his bones. He has heard tell of a ruined chapel, or an old church, no one is sure, only that it lies disused and holy, far away from prying eyes. Perhaps there he will find it. Last night Sir Perceval dreamed of the Holy Grail borne on a shaft of sunlight moving towards him. He reached out crying but his hands were full of thorns and he was awake. Tonight, bitten and bruised, he dreams of Arthur's court, where he was the darling, the favourite. He dreams of his hounds and his falcon, his stable and his faithful friends. His friends are dead now. Dead or dying. He dreams of Arthur sitting on a wide stone step, holding his head in his hands, Sir Perceval falls to his knees to clasp his lord, but his lord is a tree covered in ivy. He wakes, his face bright with tears.

When the pastor came round the next morning, I felt better. We had a cup of tea, the three of us; I think my mother told a joke. It was settled.

'Shall I book you in for the holiday then?' the pastor asked, fiddling for his diary. 'She's expecting you, but it's only polite.'

'How's Elsie?' This was bothering me.

The pastor frowned and said that last night had upset her more than they had realized. She had gone back into hospital for a check-up.

'Will she be all right?'

My mother pointed out that was for the Lord to decide, and we had other things to think about. The pastor smiled gently, and asked again when we wanted to go.

'I'm not going.'

He told me I'd need a rest after the struggle. That my mother needed a rest.

'She can go. I'm leaving the church, so you can forget the rest.'

They were dumbfounded. I held on tight to the little brown pebble and hoped they'd go away. They didn't. They reasoned and pleaded and stormed and took a break and came back. They even offered me my Bible class, though under supervision. Finally the pastor shook his head and declared me one of the people in Hebrews, to whom it is impossible to speak the truth. He asked me one last time:

'Will you repent?'

'No.' And I stared at him till he looked away. He took my mother off into the parlour for half an hour. I don't know what they did in there, but it didn't matter; my mother had painted the white roses red and now she claimed they grew that way.

'You'll have to leave,' she said. 'I'm not havin' demons here.'

Where could I go? Not to Elsie's she was too sick, and no one in the church would really take the risk. If I went to Katy's there would be problems for her, and all my relatives, like most relatives, were revolting.

'I don't have anywhere to go,' I argued, following her into the kitchen.

'The Devil looks after his own,' she threw back, pushing me out.

I knew I couldn't cope, so I didn't try. I would let the feeling out later, when it was safe. For now, I had to be hard and white. In the frosty days, in the winter, the ground is white, then the sun rises, and the frosts melt ...

Further reading

James Baldwin, *Go Tell it on the Mountain* (1954)

Kiran Desai, *Hullaballoo in the Guava Orchard* (1998)

Patrick McCabe, *Breakfast on Pluto* (1998)

Alice Walker, *The Color Purple* (1983)

Questions

AO1: Developing an informed response to the text

- Make notes about what is happening in the extract.

- What does the extract tell us about the thoughts and feelings of the characters – Jeanette, her mother, her pastor, her society – towards people outside of the mainstream, dominant culture?

AO2: Understanding how structure, form and language shape meaning

- Explore the narrative viewpoints and structure of the extract.

- What do you notice about Winterson's choice of language and its effect?

AO3: Exploring connections, comparisons and the interpretations of other readers

- Consider the extract in terms of subject matter and style.

- What do you notice within the extract about the relationships between the characters, particularly between the mother and daughter?

- Compare it with any other modern literature you have read about a struggle for identity on the subject of growing up and leaving home.

- How far do you think the extract celebrates the identities of young people, especially lesbian or gay, as part of struggle and conflict?

AO4: Understanding the significance and influence of contexts

- What do you notice about the ways Winterson is influenced by and uses the context of the struggle for identity in modern literature?

- How do you think a 21st-century reader's response to such writing is shaped?

The immigrant outsider

This type of novel focuses on the concept of newcomers as outcasts. Here, it is more a case of society needing to grow up and achieve self-realisation. This is rarely the outcome, although some characters may represent progress in social attitudes to changing societies. The hero/heroines try to fit in to the new society, despite constant rejection and persecution. Such novels narrate attempts to cope with the new culture and its rules, which are often portrayed as prejudicial. This genre is particularly suited to tales of colonial and post-colonial migration, especially to the mother country of the empire from the former colonies. The dream chased is the promise of a better, richer, fairer life, although this is rarely the outcome for the beleaguered immigrant characters. Maintaining identity and forging new ones is a focus of 'immigrant outsider' novels. Themes of 'returning' are often explored, with the idea that there may be nothing or no one to go home for.

This extract is taken from different sections of *Small Island* by Andrea Levy (2004). This edition is published by Headline.

This extract is where Gilbert, a Jamaican man stationed with the British RAF in London during World War Two, has gone to the pictures to see a film with Queenie, an English woman whose husband is stationed abroad, and Arthur, her father, who is shell-shocked from World War One and does not speak.

Extract B

Pages 183–6 from the section 'Before', Chapter 17, entitled 'Gilbert'

'What's the problem, Gilbert?' she asked. So tumultuous was the music she looked to Arthur, fearful he might have thrown himself to the ground. 'He has to go up to the back,' the usherette said.

'But there are seats here,' Queenie responded.

'I just tell her that – she say it's the rules.'

'Rules, what rules?' Queenie asked.

I quieted her with a hand placed gently on her arm – I would take care of this myself. 'You sit, Queenie – I soon come.' Then, turning to this usherette, I asked the same question, 'What rules?'

It was then she took her torch to shine its searchlight beam up to the back rows of the picture house. For the briefest moment she ran her light along the faces sitting there. Queenie would not have seen: she would have asked, 'What? What are you showing me?' But I saw. As startling as exposing a horde of writhing cockroaches, that light, although searching for only a second, gave me an image that seared indelible into my mind's eye. It flashed across lines of black faces, illuminating the heedless and impassive features of a large group of black GIs enjoying the film.

'You have to sit with them.'

'Madam,' I told her, 'I am not an American. I am with the British RAF.'

'You're coloured.'

Queenie was back. 'What are you talking about?'

'Coloured, he's coloured.' She shone the light once more to the back rows, this time holding it there so Queenie, puzzled at first, would gradually come to see. Caught by the beam, some of the men seemed to awaken with the light.

'This is England,' I said. 'This is not America. We do not do this in England. I will sit anywhere I please.'

'Well, we do it here. It's the rules. All niggers—' She stopped and began again. 'All coloureds up the back rows.'

'Why?' Queenie asked.

'Because that's their seats.'

'No! Why do coloured people have to sit where you say?'

'Our other customers don't like to sit next to coloureds.'

'Who are these other customers? Yanks?' I asked.

'They won't sit next to you.'

'What other customers? Who?' I was shouting now.

'They don't like to be all mixed up.'

'Americans?'

'Not just Yanks. Anyone.'

'We'll sit next to him – he can sit between us,' Queenie offered. I wanted to be pleased that this sweet Englishwoman was speaking up for me. But, come, Queenie's good intentions were entirely missing the point.

'In this country I sit where I like.'

'Then you'll have to go. It's up the back or nowhere.'

'Madam, there is no Jim Crow in this country.'

'Who?'

'Jim Crow.'

'Well, if he's coloured he'll have to sit at the back.'

'Segregation, madam, there is no segregation in this country. I will sit wherever I like in this picture house. And those coloured men at the back should have been allowed to sit wherever they so please. This is England, not Alabama.'

Like air escaping from an overheating machine, the sound of shushing came at us from all around. Along with the impatient 'Be quiet, some of us want to watch the film.'

'You'll have my job. I don't make the rules. Other coloureds don't make such a fuss. It's up the back or nothing.'

And I told her, 'Madam, I will neither go to the back nor will I leave. My friends and I intend to enjoy the film from this spot.'

My heart thumped so I feared the toe-tapping beat would be told to shush. Cha, nah, man – is bareface check! We fighting the persecution of the Jew, yet even in my RAF blue my coloured skin can permit anyone to treat me as less than a man. I turned my back on the usherette, indicated for Queenie to sit and went to take my seat next to her.

It was an American voice – solid as thunder – coming from a few rows in front that called out to me, 'Sit, where you're told, boy.'

I ignored it.

'Hey nigger, I said sit where the lady tells ya.'

I sat myself beside Queenie. This GI stood up – his silhouette rising like a mortal tempest before the screen.

'Look, we don't want any trouble,' the now fearful usherette pleaded.

'Nigger, do as you're told,' the GI shouted.

'And you can put a sock in it,' Queenie replied, standing up. Her fierce finger wagging.

'Nigger, move.'

'And you can shut up with your nigger,' Queenie said, 'I prefer them to you any day.'

A woman's voice called, 'You tell 'em love – ruddy loud-mouth Yanks.' I did not have to look, I could feel the edgy stirring in the back of the picture house as someone shouted, 'Shut up, whitey. We ain't taking that no more.'

Further reading

Hanif Kureishi, *Buddha of Suburbia* (1990)

Ann Michaels, *Fugitive Pieces* (1996)

Zadie Smith, *White Teeth* (2000)

Questions

AO1: Developing an informed response to the text

■ Make notes about what is happening in the extract.

■ What does the extract tell us about the thoughts and feelings of the characters – Gilbert, Queenie, the usherette – towards people outside of the dominant culture?

AO2: Understanding how structure, form and language shape meaning

■ Explore the effect of the structure and change in narrative viewpoint of the extract.

■ What do you notice about Levy's choice of language and its effect?

■ Consider the tone and setting within the extract. What is the effect of these on the reader?

AO3: Exploring connections, comparisons and the interpretations of other readers

■ What do you notice within the extract about the relationships between the characters, particularly Queenie and Gilbert?

■ Compare it with any other modern literature you have read about a struggle for identity on the subject of fitting into a new society and culture.

■ How far do you think this extract represents the struggle for identity of black immigrants to Britain?

■ It has been said that racist attitudes towards people from other cultures are a thing of the past, and that the English literature which perpetuates such stereotypes is irrelevant and out of date. How far does this view apply to *Small Island*?

AO4: Understanding the significance and influence of contexts

■ What do you notice about the ways Levy is influenced by and uses the context of the struggle for identity in modern literature?

■ The novel was written in 2004 about society in Britain during and shortly after the 1940s. How do you think a 21st-century reader's response to such writing is shaped?

The local outsider

This type of novel features a hero, heroine or central character (or characters) who does not belong within the dominant culture of their own society or country. As local outsiders and members of the 'underclass', they are presented as ghettoised and unable to gain social acceptance or status in any meaningful way respected by the dominant culture. This narrative viewpoint is well employed to document the struggles for identity of a minority or subjugated race, culture or sexuality within an otherwise potentially progressive society – making the isolation all the keener for the central character within the narrative. A sense of 'suffering' is key within that person, as she or he is forbidden to integrate. Attempts at resistance may range from noble and fruitful to desperate and destructive, depending on the era and context of the novel. Very often the novel of the local outsider charts the downfall of a person whose reaction to rejection and persecution is severely punished by the prevailing society.

These extracts are taken from different novels with contrasting cultures and settings. Extract C1 is from *Native Son* by Richard Wright (1940) and presents the central character of Bigger Thompson, a young African American man from a poverty-stricken family living in Chicago, a racially segregated American city of the 1930s. This edition was published by Vintage in 2000 and has a very useful introduction by the author and the writer Caryl Phillips.

Extract C1

Pages 49–52, from Book One, Fear

> The plane was gone from the sky and the white plumes of floating smoke were thinly spread, vanishing. Because he was restless and had time on his hands, Bigger yawned again and hoisted his arms high above his head.
> 'Nothing ever happens,' he complained.

'What you want to happen?'

'Anything,' Bigger said with a wide sweep of his dingy palm, a sweep that included all the possible activities of the world.

Then their eyes were riveted; a slate-colored pigeon swooped down to the middle of the steel car tracks and began strutting to and fro with ruffled feathers, its fat neck bogging with regal pride. A streetcar rumbled forward and the pigeon rose swiftly through the air on wings stretched so taut and sheer that Bigger could see the gold of the sun through the translucent tips. He tilted his head and watched the slate-colored bird flap and wheel out of sight over the edge of a high roof.

'Now, if I could only do that,' Bigger said.

Gus laughed.

'Nigger, you nuts.'

'I reckon we the only things in this city that can't go where we want to go and do what we want to do.'

'Don't think about it,' Gus said.

'I can't help it.'

'That's why you feeling like something awful's going to happen to you,' Gus said. 'You think too much.'

'What in hell can a man do?' Bigger asked, turning to Gus.

'Get drunk and sleep it off.'

'I can't. I'm broke.'

Bigger crushed his cigarette and took out another one and offered the package to Gus. They continued smoking. A huge truck swept past, lifting scraps of white paper into the sunshine; the bits settled down slowly.

'Gus?'

'Hunh?'

'You know where the white folks live?'

'Yeah,' Gus said, pointing eastward. 'Over across the "line"; over there on Cottage Grove Avenue.'

'Naw; they don't,' Bigger said.

'What you mean?' Gus asked, puzzled. 'Then, where do they live?'

Bigger doubled his fist and struck his solar plexus.

'Right down here in my stomach,' he said.

Gus looked at Bigger searchingly, then away, as though ashamed.

'Yeah I know what you mean,' he whispered.

'Every time I think of 'em, I feel 'em,' Bigger said.

'Yeah; and in your chest and throat, too,' Gus said.

'It's like fire.'

'And sometimes you can't hardly breathe…'

Bigger's eyes were wide and placid, gazing into space.

'That's when I feel like something awful's going to happen to me…' Bigger paused, narrowed his eyes. 'Naw; it ain't like something going to happen to me. It's like I was going to do something I can't help…'

'Yeah!' Gus said with uneasy eagerness. His eyes were full of a look compounded of fear and admiration for Bigger.

'Yeah; I know what you mean. It's like you going to fall and don't know where you going to land.'

Indeed Bigger did do something – he accidentally murdered a white woman who was the daughter of the rich landlord of the rat-infested room he shared with his family. He was subsequently sentenced to death for his crime, leaving the novel via death row.

■ Questions

AO1: Developing an informed response to the text

■ Make notes about what is happening in the extract.

■ What does the extract tell us about Bigger's thoughts and feelings towards the dominant culture?

AO2: Understanding how structure, form and language shape meaning

■ Explore the effect of the narrative viewpoint of the extract.

■ What do you notice about Wright's choice of language and its effect?

■ Consider the tone and use of an urban setting. Explore the use of the pigeon metaphor.

AO3: Exploring connections, comparisons and the interpretations of other readers

■ Compare the use of subject matter and style with those in Extract C2.

■ Compare this to any other modern literature you have read about a struggle for identity on the subject of racism within (American) society.

■ Wright claimed that in Bigger he created a hero who 'would not offer his white readers the opportunity of an escape into either pity or sympathy'. He wanted to 'make them face the difficult facts of African American life for themselves, and encourage them to accept their complicity in the misery of this American underclass.' How far do you think this is true of the extract you have read?

■ The African American writer James Baldwin criticises *Native Son* 'as more political tract than novel ... with an agenda that the author has somewhat clumsily imposed upon his characters.' How far do you agree with this view of *Native Son*?

AO4: Understanding the significance and influence of contexts

■ What do you notice about the ways Wright is influenced by and uses the contexts of the struggle for identity in modern literature?

■ The novel was written over 65 years ago. How relevant do you find the novel as a social commentary in the 21st century?

Extracts C2 and C3 are taken from *The God of Small Things* (1997) by Arundhati Roy. This edition was published by Harper Perennial in 2004. Set in the southern India of the 1960s to 1990s, the dustcover says that it 'explores the tragic fate of a family which "tampered with the laws that lay down who should be loved, and how".'

Extract C2 features the episode where the police come to arrest Velutha, a Paravan man, an Untouchable, who has broken the caste law by having a sexual relationship with Ammu (Margaret), a Christian caste woman, a Touchable, when she was even forbidden to touch him or to walk across a floor in his footsteps. The event is witnessed by her children, Esthappen (Estha) and Rahel.

Extract C2

Pages 307–11 from Chapter 17, The History House

They woke Velutha with their boots.

Esthappen and Rahel woke to the shout of sleep surprised by shattered kneecaps.

Screams died in them and floated belly up, like dead fish. Cowering on the floor, rocking between dread and disbelief, they realized that the man being beaten was Velutha. Where had he come from? Why had the policemen brought him here?

They heard the thud of wood on flesh. Boot on bone. On teeth. The muffled grunt when a stomach is kicked in. The muted crunch of skull on cement. The gurgle of blood on a man's breath when his lung is torn by the jagged end of a broken rib.

Blue-lipped and dinner-plate eyed, they watched, mesmerised by something that they sensed but didn't understand: the absence of caprice in what the policemen did. The abyss where anger should have been. The sober, steady brutality, the economy of it all.

They were opening a bottle.

Or shutting a tap.

Cracking an egg to make an omelette.

The twins were too young to know that these were only history's henchmen. Sent to square the books and collect the dues from those who broke its laws. Impelled by feelings that were primal yet paradoxically wholly impersonal. Feelings of contempt born of inchoate, unacknowledged fear – civilization's fear of nature, men's fear of women, power's fear of powerlessness.

Man's subliminal urge to destroy what he could neither subdue nor deify.

Men's needs.

What Esthappen and Rahel witnessed that morning, though they didn't know it then, was a clinical demonstration in controlled conditions (this was not war after all, or genocide) of human nature's pursuit of ascendancy. Structure. Order. Complete monopoly. It was human history, masquerading as God's Purpose, revealing herself to an under-age audience.

There was nothing accidental about what happened that morning. Nothing incidental. It was no stray mugging or personal settling of scores. There was an era imprinting itself on those who lived in it.

History in live performance.

If they hurt Velutha more than they intended to, it was only because any kinship, any connection between themselves and him, any implication that if nothing else, at least biologically he was a fellow creature – had been severed long ago. They were not arresting a man, they were exorcising fear. They had no instrument to calibrate how much punishment he could take. No means of gauging how much or permanently they had damaged him.

Unlike the custom of rampaging religious mobs or conquering armies running riot, that morning in the Heart of Darkness the posse of Touchable Policemen acted with economy, not frenzy. Efficiency, not anarchy. Responsibility not hysteria. They didn't tear out his hair or burn him alive. They didn't hack off his genitals and stuff them in his mouth. They didn't rape him. Or behead him.

After all, they were not battling an epidemic. They were merely inoculating a community against an outbreak.

In the back verandah of the History House, as the man they loved was smashed and broken, Mrs Eapen and Mrs Rajagopalan, Twin Ambassadors of God-knows-what, learned two new lessons.

Lesson Number One:

Blood barely shows on a Black Man (Dum dum)

And

Lesson Number Two:

It smells, though.

Sicksweet.

Like old roses on a breeze. (Dum dum)

'Madiyo?' one of History's Agents asked.

'Madi aayirikkum,' another replied.

Enough?

Enough.

They stepped away from him. Craftsmen assessing their work. Seeking aesthetic distance.

Their Work, abandoned by God and History, by Marx, by Man, by Woman and (in the hours to come) by Children, lay folded on the floor. He was conscious, but he wasn't moving.

His skull was fractured in three places. His nose and both his cheekbones were smashed, leaving his face pulpy, undefined. The blow to his mouth had split open his upper lip and broken six teeth, three of which were embedded in his lower lip, hideously inverting his beautiful smile. Four of his ribs were splintered, one had pierced his left lung, which was what made him bleed from his mouth. The blood on his breath bright red. Fresh. Frothy. His lower intestine was ruptured and haemorrhaged, the blood collected in his abdominal cavity. His spine was damaged in two places, the concussion had paralysed his right arm and resulted in a loss of control over his bladder and rectum. Both his knee caps were shattered.

Still they brought out the handcuffs.

Cold.

With the sourmetal smell. Like steel bus-rails and the bus conductor's hands from holding them. That was when they noticed his painted nails. One of them held them up and waved their fingers coquettishly at the others. They laughed. 'What's this?' in a high falsetto. 'AC-DC?'

One of them flicked at his penis with his stick. 'Come on, show us your special secret. Show us how big it gets when you blow it up.' Then he lifted his boot (with millipedes curled into its sole) and brought it down with a soft thud.

They locked his arms across his back.

Click.

And click.

Below a Lucky Leaf. An autumn leaf at night. That made the monsoons come on time.

He had goosebumps where the handcuffs touched his skin. It isn't him,' Rahel whispered to Estha. 'I can tell. It's his twin brother. Urumban. From Kochi.'

Unwilling to seek refuge in fiction, Estha said nothing.

Someone was speaking to them. A kind Touchable police-man. Kind to his kind.

'Mon, Mol, are you all right? Did he hurt you?'

And not together, but almost, the twins replied in a whisper.

'Yes. No.'

'Don't worry. You're safe with us now.'

Inevitably, the narrative reveals that the character Velutha did not live beyond these events in the novel. The final chapter, Chapter 21, poignantly recalls him; his place in nature, his relationship with Ammu, the first time they made love together, his part in *The God of Small Things*. Extract C3, below, is towards the end of the novel.

Extract C3

Pages 333–4, from Chapter 21, The Cost of Living

When he saw her the detonation almost drowned him. It took all his strength to stay afloat. He trod water, standing in the middle of a dark river.

She didn't see the knob of his head bobbing over the dark river. He could have been anything. A floating coconut. In any case she wasn't looking. Her head was buried in her arms.

He watched her. He took his time.

Had he known that he was about to enter a tunnel whose only egress was his own annihilation, would he have turned away?

Perhaps.

Perhaps not.

Who can tell?

He began to swim towards her. Quietly. Cutting through the water with no fuss. He had almost reached the bank when she looked up and saw him. His feet touched the muddy riverbed. As he rose from the dark river and walked up the stone steps, she saw that the world they stood on was his. That he belonged to it. That it belonged to him. The water. The mud. The trees. The fish. The stars. He moved so easily through it. As she watched him she understood the quality of his beauty. How his labour had shaped him. How the wood he fashioned had fashioned him. Each plank he planed, each nail he drove, each thing he made, had moulded him. Had left its stamp on him. Had given him his strength, his supple grace.

He wore a thin white cloth around his loins, looped between his dark legs. He shook the water from his hair. She could see his smile in the dark. His white, sudden smile that he had carried with him from boyhood into manhood. His only luggage…

■ **Further reading**

Nadime Gordimer, *July's People* (1981)

Radclyffe Hall, *The Well of Loneliness* (1928)

Zora Neale Hurston, *Their Eyes were Watching God* (1937)

Questions

AO1: Developing an informed response to the text

■ Make notes about what is happening in each extract.

■ What does each extract tell us about the thoughts and feelings of the characters – the police, Ammu, her children – towards people outside of the dominant culture?

AO2: Understanding how structure, form and language shape meaning

■ Explore the effect of the change in narrative voice in each extract.

■ What do you notice about Roy's choice of language and its effect?

■ Consider the changes in tone and setting within and across the two extracts. What is the effect of these changes on the reader?

■ Extract C3, from the final chapter of the novel, describes events and feelings that happened not only before the events of Extract C2, an earlier chapter, but within the whole narrative structure several years earlier than the opening of the novel. What could be the purpose of this use of a split narrative?

AO3: Exploring connections, comparisons and the interpretations of other readers

■ Compare the use of subject matter and style across the extracts.

■ What do you notice within and across the two extracts about the relationships between the characters, in particular between (i) Velutha and Ammu, (ii) Velutha and the children, (iii) the children and the police?

■ Compare them with any other modern literature you have read about a struggle for identity on the subject of forbidden love and ethnic inequality and persecution.

■ How far do you think these extracts conform to the genre of a love story?

■ Meera Syal's review said: 'there were times I had to stop reading this novel because I feared so much for the characters, or I had to re-read a phrase or a page to memorise its grace'. How do you respond to this idea after reading the extracts?

AO4: Understanding the significance and influence of contexts

■ What do you notice about the ways Roy is influenced by and uses the context of the struggle for identity in modern literature?

■ The setting is late 20th-century Indian post-colonial, hierarchical society. What relevance can the novel offer to its 21st-century readers?

Identity in crisis: leaving the mainstream

This type of novel concerns a hero or heroine who lacks sympathy with his or her social or local context. Unable to cope with the practical and emotional realities of day-to-day life and the concept of human living, the central character rejects the values of the society around her or him and chooses to withdraw. This withdrawal from society can be presented as either or both mental and literal. This motivation for withdrawal may range from character response to a trauma or a complete lack of identification with the material world and its beliefs and priorities.

Extract D is from *Slaughterhouse 5* (1969) by Kurt Vonnegut. This edition was published by Vintage in 2000. This extract is taken from the beginning of the novel where the hero, Billy, is first presented to the reader. Vonnegut uses this initial episode to prepare the reader for the split narrative which follows throughout the novel.

Extract D

Pages 17–20, from Chapter 2

LISTEN:

BILLY PILGRIM has come unstuck in time.

Billy has gone to sleep a senile widower and awakened on his wedding day. He has walked through a door in 1955 and come out another one in 1941. He has gone back through that door to find himself in 1963. He has seen his birth and death many times, he says, and pays random visits to all the events in between.

HE SAYS,

Billy is spastic in time, has no control over where he is going next, and the trips aren't necessarily fun. He is in a state of stage fright, he says, because he never knows what part of his life he is going to have to act in next.

Billy was born in 1922 in Ilium, New York, the only child of a barber there. He was a funny-looking youth – tall and weak and shaped like a bottle of Coca-Cola. He graduated from Ilium High School in the upper third of his class, and attended night sessions at the Ilium School of Optometry for one semester before being drafted for military service in the Second World War. His father died in a hunting accident during the war. So it goes.

Billy saw service with the infantry in Europe, and was taken prisoner by the Germans. After his honorable discharge from the Army in 1945, Billy again enrolled in the Ilium School of Optometry. During his senior year there, he became engaged to the daughter of the founder and owner of the school, and then suffered a mild nervous collapse.

He was treated in a veteran's hospital near Lake Placid, and was given shock treatments and released. He married his fiancée, finished his education, and was set up in business in Ilium by his father-in-law. Ilium is a particularly good city for optometrists because the General Gorge and Foundry Company is there. Every employee is required to own a pair of safety glasses, and to wear them in areas where manufacturing is going on. GF&F has sixty-eight thousand employees in Ilium. That calls for a lot of lenses and a lot of frames. Frames are where the money is.

Billy became rich. He had two children, Barbara and Robert. In time, his daughter Barbara married another optometrist, and Billy set him up in business. Billy's son Robert had a lot of trouble in high school, but then he joined the famous Green Berets. He straightened out, became a fine young man, and he fought in Vietnam.

Early in 1968, a group of optometrists, with Billy among them, chartered an airplane to fly them from Ilium to an international convention of optometrists in Montreal. The plane crashed on top of Sugarbush Mountain, in Vermont. Everybody was killed but Billy. So it goes.

While Billy was recuperating in a hospital in Vermont, his wife died accidentally of carbon-monoxide poisoning. So it goes.

When Billy finally got home to Ilium after the airplane crash, he was quiet for a while. He had a terrible scar across the top of his skull. He didn't resume practice. He had a housekeeper. His daughter came over almost every day.

Fig. 5.2 *Billy Pilgrim from the film adaptation of* Slaughterhouse 5

And then, without any warning, Billy went to New York City, and got on an all-night radio program devoted to talk. He told about having come unstuck in time. He said, too, that he had been kidnapped by a flying saucer in 1967. The saucer was from the planet Tralfamadore, he said. He was taken to Tralfamadore, where he was displayed naked in a zoo, he said. He was mated there with a former Earthling movie star named Montana Wildhack.

Some night owls in Ilium heard Billy on the radio, and one of them called Billy's daughter Barbara. Barbara was upset. She and her husband went down to New York and brought Billy home. Billy insisted mildly that everything he had said on the radio was true. He said he had been kidnapped by the Tralfamadorians on the night of his daughter's wedding. He hadn't been missed, he said, because the Tralfamadorians had taken him through a time warp, so that he could be on Tralfamadore for years, and still be away from Earth for only a microsecond.

Another month went by without incident, and then Billy wrote a letter to the *Ilium News Leader*, which the paper published. It described the creatures from Tralfamadore.

The letter said that they were two feet high, and green, and shaped like plumber's friends. Their suction cups were on the ground, and their shafts, which were extremely flexible, usually pointed to the sky. At the top of each shaft was a little hand with a green eye in its palm. The creatures were friendly, and they could see in four dimensions. They pitied Earthlings for being able to see only three. They had many wonderful things to teach Earthlings, especially about time. Billy promised to tell what some of those wonderful things were in his next letter.

Billy was working on his second letter when the first letter was published. The second letter started out like this:

'The most important thing I learned on Tralfamadore was that when a person dies he only appears to die. He is still very much alive in the past, so it is very silly for people to cry at his funeral. All moments, past, present, and future, always have existed, always will exist. The Tralfamadorians can look at all the different moments just the way we can look at a stretch of the Rocky Mountains, for instance. They can see how permanent all the moments are, and they can look at any moment that interests them. It is just an illusion we have here on Earth that one moment follows another one, like beads on a string, and that once a moment is gone it is gone forever.

'When a Tralfamadorian sees a corpse, all he thinks is that the dead person is in bad condition in that particular moment, but that the same person is just fine in plenty of other moments. Now, when I myself hear that someone is dead, I simply shrug and say what the Tralfamadorians say about dead people, which is "So it goes." '

Questions

AO1: Developing an informed response to the text

■ Make notes about what is happening in the extract.

■ What does the extract tell us about the thoughts and feelings of the characters – Billy Pilgrim and his daughter – towards the relevance of accepting social norms of behaviour and attitude?

AO2: Understanding how structure, form and language shape meaning

■ Explore the effect of the narrative voice in the extract.

■ What do you notice about the writer's choice of language and its effect?

■ Consider the importance of the tone and overall setting (post-war small-town America) in the extract. What is the effect on the reader?

■ How does the writer use the specific setting (of Tralfamadore) as a metaphor?

AO3: Exploring connections, comparisons and the interpretations of other readers

■ Compare the extract with any other modern literature you have read about a struggle for identity on the subject of leaving the mainstream culture and even a recognisable reality.

■ How far do you think this extract conforms to the genre of a dystopia?

■ After reading the extracts, how do you respond to the idea that this novel presents the behaviour of a victim, who is incapable of coherent thought and contributing to his society?

AO4: Understanding the significance and influence of contexts

■ What do you notice about the ways the writer is influenced by and uses the context of the struggle for identity in modern literature?

■ The science-fiction context in *Slaughterhouse 5* can be viewed as a product of its time – a preoccupation with space travel and aliens in the 1950s and 1960s. What relevance can this novel offer to 21st-century readers whose lives may never come into contact with any of the realities described in the narrative?

Further reading

Chinua Achebe, *Things Fall Apart* (1958)

Kiran Desai, *Hullaballoo in the Guava Orchard* (1998)

Robert Tressell, *The Ragged-Trousered Philanthropists* (1914)

💡 *Summary*

In this chapter we have surveyed novels about the struggle for identity in modern literature from different narrative viewpoints. As you keep a record of your reading, you will need to explore the ways different writers approach the **shared context,** and ask yourself the following questions:

■ Through whose eyes and to what effect do we experience this tale?

■ Whose tale is it?

■ What kind of tale do they tell us?

■ What sub-genres are used?

Tackling wider reading in drama

Aims of the chapter:

- Introduces a selection of extracts from plays about 'The Struggle for Identity in Modern Literature', as part of the Specification's wider reading requirement.

- Considers the different techniques and sub-genres used by dramatists writing about struggles for identity to create dramatic effects.

- Explains how the Assessment Objectives can be applied to the drama extracts you have studied.

- Helps you begin to form your own ideas about the key features of content and style in plays about 'The Struggle for Identity in Modern Literature'.

- Explores connections between the drama extracts and considers the importance of the context of writing about struggles for identity.

Link

For some historical context to set the scene for modern prose, see pp41–43.

Introduction

When you attempt the context question in the AS exam, your answer should include some relevant references to plays you have studied, so it is important that you are familiar with a range of plays on struggles for identity. As well as studying the scripts of plays, you will find it helpful to experience them in performance. You should try to see some of these plays live on stage – or at least on film or DVD.

In this chapter we are going to look in detail at seven extracts from five different plays.

If you have read Chapters 4 and 5, particularly the introductions on historical and political background affecting the modern era of the 20th and early 21st centuries, then hopefully you will have started to grasp the nature of this unit – The Struggle for Identity in Modern Literature – and what ties these texts and extracts together.

Structure of the chapter

This chapter includes:

1 Some background on the genre of modern drama
2 Extracts and activities.

Some background on the genre of modern drama

Links with the genres of poetry and prose fiction

Like the poetry, and the prose, we can consider drama as a form that can convey struggles for identity as essentially personal, focused on the concept of 'the self', or essentially communal, focused on issues that are 'social'.

We also considered in Chapter 5 how tricky it is to categorise the novel form as belonging to only one sub-genre of narrative, so we looked at novels from the narrative viewpoints of different types of outsiders. These observations can also apply to drama.

Differences from the genres of poetry and prose fiction

However, drama does have some differences from poetry and prose which are to do with how we have used this form for the last century. It *is* easier to consider drama from the perspective of its sub-genres. In this chapter, we focus on three important dramatic sub-genres and the 'merging' that followed them. We consider ideas and extracts from plays which belong to:

- the documentary approach – the drama of social realism
- the suspension of disbelief – the Theatre of the Absurd
- political drama – the theatre of alienation
- the recent merge – late 20th- and 21st-century approaches.

The documentary approach – the drama of social realism

Modern drama, despite appearing to be a type of narrative in that it might tell a story like prose fiction, can be considered to employ more of a **documentary approach** than either of the other two genres. It often focuses on reporting and exploring single or grouped events to replicate what the dramatist sees as a concern or interest in the world around her or him. The form of staging dynamic dialogue and actions before a live audience, over a few hours, has an intensity that can be compared to watching a live TV news event or report being documented to a similarly watching audience. Audiences believe the news to be real, even though it is filtered through a medium of distance, perception (as it is, of course, edited, even when live) and sometimes even time. This sense of viewing 'real' events influences an audience's experience of theatre.

Yet drama, like poetry and prose fiction, is clearly still an invented, literary form. The dramatist is not compelled to tell truths, unlike the responsibility of the news. Drama does seem to favour explicit presentations of the wider social issues more heavily, and it could even be argued more reliably or faithfully, than the other two genres, as it is an 'events/action-propelled' genre. Even when the focus is 'the self', many dramatists choose inevitably to set that self, and the character/s through whom this is conveyed, in a social setting which suggests a larger communal reality, something believable for many people.

Consequently, modern dramas about an individual's 'coming of age' are rarer, while dramas of **social realism**, a variety of **naturalism**, abound. We will consider the ideas and forms of social realism in Extract A, from Sean O'Casey's *Juno and the Paycock*, and Extract D, from Lorraine Hansberry's *A Raisin in the Sun*, later in this chapter.

The suspension of disbelief – the Theatre of the Absurd

Interestingly, drama is often seen as the genre which, contrary to the above documentary approach, allows for the imagination, fantasy and magic to flourish. We enter the world of the theatre in hushed tones, with a darkened forum and a silent audience. Here we are encouraged to **suspend our disbelief** about what is real or possible and what is not. Here, we do not need to rely on our own imaginations for the conjuring of fantastic stories, settings, beings and creatures because they are moving around the stage in front of us, as large as life itself.

Through this realisation, this **realisable text**, the play seems to take on a reality that you could argue is harder to take from poetry and prose fiction, which rely on imagining what it is like to be someone else rather than, as with drama, watching an actor *being* a character, being someone with a potential to *be real*. We accept that it is happening, or could happen, because we are watching it. 'Seeing is believing' – and that makes anything credible in theatre, even the extremely strange and unlikely realities far removed from a documentary style of drama.

It is from this perspective that we can consider the **Theatre of the Absurd**, which comes out of the existentialist movement. This type of play is the ideal place to explore the concept of the 'self' without, or outside of, a wider social setting.

Absurdism is the greatest dramatic contrast to the social realist plays of the 20th century. We will consider this idea and use of form in Extract C, from Samuel Beckett's play *Endgame*, later in the chapter.

Political theatre – the theatre of alienation

While the sub-genres of social realist and absurdist dramas dominated modern drama, a different movement gathered pace, the **theatre of alienation**. The idea behind this form is that the audience is made to remember that what we are watching on the stage is just that – staged. We are reminded that it is not real and warned that it is misleading to use a documentary approach, which is at best only a representation of reality. The theatre of alienation demands that drama is a highly transparent construct, designed to promote a set of social ideas, with the characters used merely as tools to communicate the playwright's purpose, not as interesting in themselves.

It is designed to challenge us. It goes beyond social realism and suggests that crying in a cathartic climax at some poor person's tragic situation is an illusion and soon forgotten after the play is over. The purpose of this type of theatre is to provoke action beyond the performance to change the 'realities' and social situations witnessed in the theatre. In this way it is very different from the Theatre of the Absurd, which has no interest in an external reality beyond that imagined through the characters in the play.

It uses a range of simple dramatic devices to highlight the fact that the room is filled with actors, props, a script and a detached audience. It discourages sympathy and empathy with characters, in favour of an objective consideration of the moral issues under observation. This can result in a kind of alienation or detachment from the individual worries of the characters to see the bigger social picture offered to the audience.

Not surprisingly, this is a highly political style of theatre, beloved of left-wing dramatists, particularly 20th-century Marxists. The unsurpassed pioneer of the theatre of alienation is Bertolt Brecht. We will consider this in Extract B, from *Mother Courage and her Children*, later in the chapter.

The recent merge – late 20th- and 21st-century approaches

The three sub-genres above clinch the influential movements and approaches in modern drama. What happens when it has all been done before? How can our contemporary dramatists present and reflect our complicated 21st-century world? The way beyond them since the 1980s has been to merge and select from their techniques and ideas, as we saw novelists do in Chapters 3 and 5, with the legacies they have inherited.

Dramatists interested in:

■ expressing social realist concerns of contemporary events
■ employing the use of 'magic and fantasy' to enhance ideas about other realities and reasons to adopt them
■ creating a dramatic framework where characters only seem to exist in the setting created for them
■ political ideas which attract them to the non-illusory techniques employed by the theatre of alienation

can produce some hard-hitting, landmark drama. We offer you such an example in Extract E, from Tony Kushner's *Angels in America*, later in the chapter.

■ Extracts and activities

The documentary approach – the drama of social realism

Juno and the Paycock, by Sean O'Casey (1924*)*

O'Casey was the first Irish dramatist to write about ordinary Dublin life in a naturalistic way. He chose to concentrate on subject matter which depicted the cost of war for home and family. A committed nationalist, and in fact a socialist, he was also critical of the violent outcome of war and all his plays carry an anti-war or anti-conflict message. However, his main concern dramatically was to represent realistically the actual struggles of the poverty-stricken Irish working class, beleaguered and divided in this play.

Mr Boyle – Jack – spends his time drunk and sloping off from any employment, contributing very little but cynicism to this scene, and depending on the strength of Mrs Boyle – Juno – throughout the play. In a typically sympathetic presentation of women, O'Casey depicts in Juno a mother, wife and friend who is the sole provider of income, care and wisdom for her family.

This domestic situation is set in 1922 during the Irish Civil War, which, as O'Casey stresses in the drama, using Juno as a moral commentator, leads to far worse consequences than the Irish War of Independence of the year before. Here, as in the extract below, poor, working-class Irish families were enemies. Now the fighting was with each other on the streets and at home, for or against the post-colonial state which the retreating British government had created in a gruesome but predictable foreshadow of the Troubles to come. Brian Friel's play, *Making History*, one of your coursework drama texts, provides sombre echoes of its subject matter, written 60 years later. In this play, Johnny, Juno's son, knows his life hangs in the balance since he betrayed an IRA comrade, and as this is a tragedy you can predict how O'Casey concludes his drama.

Despite all this, the play is not simply a grim tale of grim folk in grim circumstances, as the extract below reveals. Tragedy such as this always has comic or light moments, essential to the drama.

Extract A

Three Dublin Plays, Juno and the Paycock (this edition was published by Faber in 2003)

From Act 2 pages 114–17

> *Boyle arranges the gramophone, and is about to start it, when voices are heard of persons descending the stairs.*
>
> **Mrs Boyle** (*warningly*) Whisht, Jack, don't put it on, don't put it on yet; this must be poor Mrs Tancred comin' down to go to the hospital – I forgot all about them bringin' the body to the church tonight. Open the door, Mary, an' give them a bit o' light.
>
> *Mary opens the door, and Mrs Tancred – a very old woman, obviously shaken by the death of her son – appears, accompanied by several neighbours. The first few phrases are spoken before they appear.*
>
> **First Neighbour** It's a sad journey we're goin' on, but God's good, an' the Republicans won't be always down.
>
> **Mrs Tancred** Ah, what good is that to me now? Whether they're up or down – it won't bring me darlin' boy from the grave.

Mrs Boyle Come in an' have a hot cup o' tay, Mrs Tancred, before you go.

Mrs Tancred Ah, I can take nothin' now, Mrs Boyle – I won't be long after him.

First Neighbour Still an' all, he died a noble death, an' we'll bury him like a king.

Mrs Tancred An' I'll go on livin' like a pauper. Ah, what's the pains I suffered bringin' him into the world to carry him to his cradle, to the pains I'm sufferin' now, carryin' him out o' the world to bring him to his grave!

Mary It would be better for you not to go at all, Mrs Tancred, but to stay at home beside the fire with some o' the neighbours.

Mrs Tancred I seen the first of him, an' I'll see the last of him.

Mrs Boyle You'd want a shawl, Mrs Tancred; it's a cowld night, an' the win's blowin' sharp.

Mrs Madigan (*rushing out*) I've a shawl above.

Mrs Tancred Me home is gone now; he was me only child, an' to think that he was lyin' for a whole night stretched out on the side of a lonely country lane, with his head, his darlin' head, that I often kissed an' fondled, half hidden in the wather of a runnin' brook. An I'm told he was the leadher of the ambush wher me nex' door neighbour, Mrs Mannin', lost her Free State soldier son.

Fig. 6.1 *An early production of* Juno and the Paycock

An' now here's the two of us oul' women, standin' one on each side of a scales o sorra', balanced be the bodies of our two dead darlin' sons.

Mrs Madigan returns, and wraps a shawl around her.

God bless you, Mrs Madigan… (*She moves slowly towards the door.*) Mother o' God, have pity on the pair of us!…O Blessed Virgin, where were you when me darlin' son was riddled with bullets, when me darlin' son was riddled with bullets!…Sacred Heart of the Crucified Jesus, take away our hearts o' stone…an' give us hearts o' flesh!…Take away this murdherin' hate…an' give us Thine own eternal love!

They pass out of the room.

Mrs Boyle (*explanatorily to Bentham*) That was Mrs Tancred of the two-pair back; her son was found, e'er yesterday, lyin' out beyant Finglas riddled with bullets. A Die-hard* he was, be all accounts. He was a nice quiet boy, but lattherly he went to hell, with his Republic first, an' Republic last an Republic over all. He often took tea with us here, in the oul days, an Johnny, there, an' him used to be always together.

Johnny Am I always to be havin' to tell you that he was no friend o' mine? I never cared for him, an' he could never stick me. It's not because he was Commandant of the Battalion that I was Quarther-Masther of, that we were friends.

Mrs Boyle He's gone now – the Lord be good to him! God help his poor oul' creature of a mother, for no matther whose friend or enemy he was, he was her poor son.

Bentham The whole thing is terrible, Mrs Boyle; but the only way to deal with a mad dog is to destroy it.

Mrs Boyle An' to think of me forgettin' about him bein' brought to the church tonight, an we singin' an' all, but it was well we hadn't the gramophone goin' anyhow.

Boyle Even if we had aself. We've nothin' to do with these things, one way or t'other. That's the Government's business, an' let them do what we're payin' them for doin'.

Mrs Boyle I'd like to know how a body's not to mind these things; look at the way they're afther leavin' the people in this very house. Hasn't the whole house, nearly, been massacred? There's young Dougherty's husband with his leg off; Mrs Travers that had her son blew up be a mine in Inchegeela, in Co. Cork; Mrs Mannin' that lost wan of her sons in ambush a few weeks ago, an' now, poor Mrs Tancred's only child gone west with his body made a colander of. Sure, if it's not our business, I don't know whose business it is.

…

Johnny For God's sake, let us have no more o' this talk.

Mrs Madigan What about Mr Boyle's song before we start th' gramophone?

*hardline IRA man

■ Questions

AO1: Developing an informed response to the text

■ What is happening in this scene?

■ What is your response to the different characters and their attitudes to Mrs Tancred's dead son and the war?

AO2: Understanding how structure, form and language shape meaning

■ What do you notice about the ways O'Casey uses the character of First Neighbour? Why is the character named in this way?

■ How does O'Casey use language? Consider the effects of the naturalistic metaphor 'gone west with his body made a colander of'.

■ Explore the ways the interaction of characters creates dramatic effects, particularly between Mrs Tancred and Mrs Mannigan, and then between the members of the Boyle family.

■ How does O'Casey use music here, as a device and as subject matter?

AO3: Exploring connections, comparisons and the interpretations of other readers

■ Compare the presentation of Juno with that of other female characters in plays about the struggle for identity

■ Compare the ways O'Casey writes about threatened family identity with other texts from your wider reading.

■ Does the presentation of Mr Boyle and Bentham find echoes in your wider reading?

■ O'Casey himself said that 'To me what is called naturalism, or even realism, isn't enough. They usually show life at its meanest and commonest, as if life never had time for a dance, a laugh, or a song.' How would you apply this view to *Juno and the Paycock*?

AO4: Understanding the significance and influence of contexts

■ Explore the ways the extract from the play uses the context of struggles for identity.

■ What does it have to tell you about the position of women?

■ What does it have to tell you about the impact of war on ideas of identity?

■ Further reading

On Irish issues:

■ Brendan Behan, *The Hostage* (1958)

■ Sean O'Casey, *The Plough and the Stars* (1926), *Shadow of a Gunman* (1923)

On heroines and central female characters:

■ Federico García Lorca, *The House of Bernarda Alba* (1936)

■ Martin Macdonagh, *Beauty Queen of Leenane* (1996)

■ Tennessee Williams, *A Streetcar Named Desire* (1947)

On the effects of war and conflict:

■ Sudha Bhuchar, *Child of the Divide* (post-1990)

■ Timberlake Wertenbaker, *Our Country's Good* (1988)

Political drama – the theatre of alienation

Mother Courage and her Children, by Bertolt Brecht (1939) (in translation from the German)

Brecht wrote *Mother Courage and her Children* at the outbreak of World War Two, while exiled from Nazi Germany, in Sweden. He created the play as a warning to Scandinavia not to join World War Two.

Following Brecht's own principles for political drama, *Mother Courage and her Children* is not set in his contemporary society, despite its clearly modern subject matter, but during the Thirty Years War of 1618–48, over three hundred years before. Brecht believed that removing serious social issues to a distant past allowed the audience to grasp the contemporary issues without the emotional distractions that might follow from staging familiar events that could cloud their judgement.

In line with the sub-genre of the theatre of alienation, in Mother Courage we experience a heroine whom we cannot admire. We follow the fortunes of Anna Fierling, nicknamed 'Mother Courage', a wily canteen woman with the Swedish Army who is determined to make her living from the war. Over the course of the play, she loses all three of her children – Swiss Cheese, Eilif and Kattrin – to the same war from which she sought to profit. We are given a sense of Courage's career and loss, but without enough time to develop sentimental feelings and empathise with any of the characters. Meanwhile, Mother Courage is not depicted as a noble character. She has no higher ideals, only profit and greed.

This is a different kind of anti-war play to O'Casey's. There is no pity or sympathy, no one weeps or cares for the dead, the suffering, the human condition. Brecht uses the historical distance to drive home a controversial point which not only would have resonated at the time of writing, but perhaps still does so now: however you behave in war it will destroy you. Here we see the dogma which says that war, as a strategy of the powerful, the ruling class or governments, rarely represents or serves the interest of the masses – in this case rural peasantry.

Extract B1

Mother Courage and her Children, adapted by the dramatist and director David Hare in 1995 for the National Theatre. This version was published by Methuen Drama in 1995.

> *Scene 4 Poland. 1629*
> *Mother Courage is waiting outside an officer's tent. The Regimental Clerk looks out of the tent.*
>
> **Regimental Clerk** I know you. You run that canteen. The one where they found that young thief. I wouldn't advise you to start making complaints.
>
> **Mother Courage** I've got to. They came and they slashed my cart with their sabres. They ruined my stock. And then they demanded a five-shilling fine. For nothing. If I didn't complain it would be like admitting I'd done something wrong.
>
> **Regimental Clerk** We're short of canteens, so we're prepared to let you go on trading. Specially if you pay a fine now and then. But if you take my advice, you'll say nothing.
>
> **Mother Courage** I'm here to complain.
>
> **Regimental Clerk** It's up to you. You must wait for the captain.
>
> *The Regimental Clerk goes back into the tent as a Young Soldier comes in aggressively, pursued by an Older Soldier.*
>
> **Young Soldier** Bouque la Madonne! Where is that bastard of a captain? Spending my money on drink and on whores! I'll kill you.
>
> **Older Soldier** For God's sake, keep quiet. You'll end up in the stocks!
>
> **Young Soldier** Come on out, you thief! I'll slice you in pieces! Come out and fight me! You stole my reward!
>
> **Older Soldier** Pull yourself together, man. You're going to get yourself killed.
>
> **Mother Courage** Is this some reward he didn't get?
>
> **Young Soldier** As God is my witness, if you don't let go of me, I'll swear I'll kill you as well.

Older Soldier He crossed a river to save the colonel's horse and then the colonel welched on the reward he'd promised. He's still young. He doesn't understand.

Mother Courage Let him go. He's not like a dog, you have to keep him tied up.

Young Soldier He's in there getting drunk! You're all trouser-shitters! I've done a great service and I want my reward!

Mother Courage Young man, don't shout at me, I've got my own problems. Save your voice, you'll need it when the captain comes. You'll need some voice left when he gets here. Else he won't be offended enough to put you in chains. I tell you, I've known a lot of shouters. It never lasts long. Half an hour's serious lung work and then you have to put them to bed.

Young Soldier I'm not going to listen. This is an injustice and injustice is something I will not endure.

Mother Courage Oh really? Gives you a problem, does it? Injustice? How long can't you put up with it for? Is an hour difficult? Or does it bug you for two? Because in the stocks, I tell you, there's this strange sort of moment when people suddenly think, oh perhaps I can put up with injustice after all.

Young Soldier Why am I listening to this rubbish? Bouque la Madonne, where's that captain?

Mother Courage You're listening to me because you know what I'm saying is true. Your anger has gone. It was only a short one. You need a long one. But long ones aren't always easy to find.

Young Soldier Are you daring to tell me I don't deserve my reward?

Mother Courage Not at all. Just the opposite. But I'm also saying your anger's too small. It won't get you anywhere. Not enough puff in it. If you had a big one, I'd be urging you on. Kill him, I'd say. I'd be telling you to do it. But if I encourage you and then you don't do it, then that's very dangerous, because, let's face it, the captain's going to start turning on me.

Older Soldier You're right. It was only a tantrum.

Young Soldier You say I'm not going to do it? Very well then, let's see.

He draws his sword dramatically. The Regimental Clerk pokes his head out.

Regimental Clerk The captain will be out in one minute. You over there, please sit down.

The Young Soldier sits. The Regimental Clerk withdraws.

Mother Courage And down he goes. What did I tell you? Armchair rebels! Sit down, they say, and we do. Nobody ever started a revolution sitting down. No, don't stand up again. Sad, but after what's happened it won't look the same. And don't be embarrassed by what I think of you. Believe me, I'm no different. They've bought us. They've bought our spirit.

Fig. 6.2 *Dame Judi Dench in a Royal Shakespeare Company production of* Mother Courage

Extract B2

Scene 12 Saxony. 1636

Later the same night (from scene 11), towards dawn. The sound of fife and drum as troops march off into the distance. In front of the cart Mother Courage is kneeling by her daughter's body. The Peasants are standing nearby, hostile to her.

...

Mother Courage Now she's asleep.

Peasant's Wife She's not asleep. You have to face it. She's dead. You must get moving. There are wolves round here. And what's worse, bandits.

Mother Courage Yes.

She gets a tarpaulin to cover the dead Kattrin.

Peasant's Wife Do you have anyone left? Who can you go to?

Mother Courage Yes I've still got Eilif. My son.

Peasant Then you must find him. We'll see she's properly buried. Don't you worry about that.

Mother Courage Money for expenses.

She has covered the body. Now she counts out money into the Peasant's hand. The Peasant and the Peasant's son shake her hand and then carry Kattrin off. The Peasant's Wife then takes her hand, bows as she leaves.

Peasant's Wife You have to get going.

Mother Courage goes to harness herself to the cart. She unrolls the cord which Kattrin until then had been pulling, takes a stick, examines it, pulls the loop of the second cord through and wedges the stick under her arm.

Mother Courage I just hope I can pull this thing by myself. It should be all right, there's not much in it.

She is ready to go.

Back to business!

A regiment passes by at the back with a pipe and drum. She starts to pull.

Hey! Take me with you!

As she sets off, the Soldiers are heard singing:
Soldiers
Nobody stays at war unless they have to
At the end you see the war has robbed us blind
Have you noticed? The war itself is endless
The money's being made by those who stay behind
Nobody wants to give us decent clothing
Shit is what we eat, and we've no pay
Yet who knows? Let's face it! Miracles may happen
Let's give this thing a spin for one more day

 Spring is here. The snow is melting
 The dead are gone. They're all at peace
 And what remains must now continue.
 That's us. Let's go. We're all that's left.

Questions

AO1: Developing an informed response to the text

- What is happening in these two scenes across the play?

- What do you learn about Mother Courage and how do you respond to her in each of the scenes?

AO2: Understanding how structure, form and language shape meaning

- Explore the ways the characters' interactions create dramatic effects. Trace particularly Mother Courage's relationship with the soldiers.

- How does Brecht make use of song and music?

- Examine the contrasting presentations of Mother Courage in the two extracts, with a particular focus on the language used.

- What do you notice about the title of the play, and the name 'Mother Courage'?

AO3: Exploring connections, comparisons and the interpretations of other readers

- Compare the presentation of the 'heroine' figure with other central female characters/heroine figures in your wider reading.

- What connections can you find in your wider reading with this picture of an unsympathetic hero? You might like to start with the presentation of Bigger in Richard Wright's *Native Son* in Chapter 5, Extract C1.

- From your reading of the extracts, how far do you agree with David Hare that 'two of the principal characters are ... abstract nouns. They are Time and War ... a director [needs to] show what they do to Mother Courage herself'?

- From your reading of these extracts, how do you respond to the idea that the play is about silencing someone with opinions, cynical and callous as they may be?

- What is your view of the play as a study of cowardice and assimilation?

AO4: Understanding the significance and influence of contexts

- How typical are these extracts of your wider reading in the drama about struggles for identity?

- What attitudes to the struggle for identity during wartime do you find in these extracts?

- What have you discovered about the role of women through Brecht's presentation here?

- Brecht takes a Marxist view that your ideology is a product of your social status. How can that context be applied to the characters and ideas in this play?

- *Mother Courage and her Children* was not performed in England until 1955. Why do you think that might be?

Further reading

Brecht contemporaries Lorca and O'Casey, as in Further reading for Extract A

21st-century stand-up performance art which removes the theatrical 'fourth wall', for example:

Claire Dowie, *Why is John Lennon Wearing a Skirt?* (1996)

Ntozake Shange, *For Colored Girls Who Have Considered Suicide When the Rainbow is Enuff* (1985)

Other political texts with Brechtian influence, but which merge sub-genres:

Caryl Churchill, *Top Girls* (1982)

Tony Kushner, *Angels in America* (1992)

💡 The suspension of disbelief – the Theatre of the Absurd

Endgame, by Samuel Beckett (1958)

Beckett rejected utterly the theatrical conventions of realism, including social realism and the documentary approach, in favour of plays that gave no quarter to social or external events, and, in some cases, not even a plot. Beckett is the champion of characters placed in settings in plays where nothing happens at all. The only 'reality' of the situation in which the absurd character appears, is a psychological reality. Despite this extremely strange and fantastic premise which underpins several of Beckett's plays, we accept and engage with the mental world of the isolated and static characters who occupy them. We do indeed suspend our disbelief.

The protagonists of *Endgame* are Hamm, an aged master, who is blind and can not stand up, and his servant Clov, who can not sit down. They exist in a tiny house by the sea, although the dialogue suggests that there is no exterior left – no sea, no sun, no clouds – hence the preoccupation with the windows in the stage directions. The two interdependent characters are in perpetual conflict. Clov always wants to leave, but never seems to be able to.

Beckett has been criticised as miserable and cynical, charting only human futility and despair, but others see his plays as very funny and optimistic. We are encouraged to see the humour; even Nell, a character from *Endgame*, says 'Nothing is funnier than unhappiness, I grant you that. ... Yes, yes, it's the most comical thing in the world.'

Extract C

This edition of *Endgame* was published by Faber in 2006.

The opening of the play. Pages 5–8

> *Bare interior.*
> *Grey light.*
> *Left and right back, high up, two small windows, curtains drawn. Front right, a door. Hanging near door, its face to wall, a picture. Front left, touching each other, covered with an old sheet, two ashbins.*
> *Centre, in an armchair on castors, covered with an old sheet, Hamm.*
> *Motionless by the door, his eyes fixed on Hamm, Clov Very red face. Brief tableau.*
>
> *Clov goes and stands under window left. Stiff, staggering walk. He looks up at window left. He turns and looks at window right. He goes and stands under window right. He looks up at window right. He turns and looks at window left. He goes out, comes back immediately with a small step-ladder, carries it over and sets it down under window left, gets up on it, draws back curtain. He gets down, takes six steps [for example] towards window right, goes back for ladder, carries it over and sets it down under window right, gets up on it, draws back curtain. He gets down, takes three steps towards window left, goes back for ladder, carries it over and sets it down under window left, gets up on it, looks out of window. Brief laugh. He gets down, takes one step towards window right, goes back for ladder, carries it over and sets it down under window right, gets up on it, looks out of window. Brief laugh. He gets down, goes with ladder towards ashbins, halts, turns, carries back ladder and sets it down under window right, goes to ashbins, removes sheet covering them, folds it over his arm. He raises one lid, stoops and looks into bin. Brief laugh. He closes lid. Same with other bin. He goes to HAMM, removes sheet covering him, folds it over his arm. In a dressing-gown, a stiff toque on his head, a large blood-stained handkerchief over his face, a whistle hanging from his neck, a rug over his knees, thick socks on his feet, HAMM seems to be asleep. CLOV looks him over. Brief laugh. He goes to door, halts, turns towards auditorium.*

Clov: [*Fixed gaze, tonelessly.*] Finished, it's finished, nearly finished, it must be nearly finished. [*Pause.*] Grain upon grain, one by one, and one day, suddenly, there's a heap, a little heap, the impossible heap. [*Pause.*] I'll go now to my kitchen, ten feet by ten feet by ten feet, and wait for him to whistle me. [*Pause.*] Nice dimensions, nice proportions, I'll lean on the table, and look at the wall, and wait for him to whistle me. [*He remains a moment motionless, then goes out. He comes back immediately, goes to window right, takes up the ladder and carries it out. Pause. Hamm stirs. He yawns under the handkerchief. He removes the handkerchief from his face. Very red face. Black glasses.*]

Hamm: Me – [*he yawns*] – to play. [*He holds the handkerchief spread out before him.*] Old stancher! [*He takes off his glasses, wipes his eyes, his face, the glasses, puts them on again, folds the handkerchief and puts it neatly in the breast-pocket of his dressing-gown. He clears his throat, joins the tips of his fingers.*] Can there be misery – [*he yawns*] – loftier than mine? No doubt. Formerly. But now? [*Pause.*] My father? [*Pause.*] My mother? [*Pause.*] My…dog? [*Pause.*] Oh I am willing to believe they suffer as much as such creatures can suffer. But does that mean their sufferings equal mine? No doubt. [*Pause.*] No, all is a – [he yawns] – bsolute, [*proudly*] the bigger a man is the fuller he is. [*Pause. Gloomily.*] And the emptier. [*He sniffs.*] Clov! [*Pause.*] No, alone. [*Pause.*] What dreams! Those forests! [Pause.] Enough, it's time it ended, in the refuge, too. [*Pause.*] And yet I hesitate, I hesitate to…to end. Yes, there it is, it's time it ended and yet I hesitate to – [*he yawns*] – to end. [*Yawns.*] God, I'm tired, I'd be better off in bed. [*He whistles. Enter CLOV immediately. He halts beside the chair.*] You pollute the air [*Pause.*] Get me ready, I'm going to bed.

Clov: I've just got you up.

Hamm: And what of it?

Clov: I can't be getting you up and putting you to bed every five minutes, I have things to do.

[*Pause.*]

Hamm: Did you ever see my eyes?

Clov: No.

Hamm: Did you never have the curiosity, while I was sleeping, to take off my glasses and look at my eyes?

Clov: Pulling back the lids? [*Pause*] No.

Hamm: One of these days I'll show them to you. [*Pause.*] It seems they've gone all white. [*Pause.*] What time is it?

Clov: The same as usual.

Hamm: [*Gesture towards window right.*] Have you looked?

Clov: Yes.

Fig. 6.3 *Still from a production of* Endgame

Further reading

Samuel Beckett, *Waiting for Godot* (1949)

Arthur Miller, *Death of a Salesman* (1949)

(While you could not claim Miller as absurdist, we are certainly required to suspend our disbelief to watch and engage with this play about the impact on a family of the hollow con of the American dream. The split-narrative technique, as described in Chapter 5, and applied here to drama, the limited plot, the claustrophobic setting, the hallucinations of the main character and the stage directions outlining the importance of futile domestic routine, all provide clear links to Beckett, Miller's contemporary, and absurdist ideas.)

Beckett influenced:

- Brian Friel, *Dancing at Lughnasa* (1990)
- Tony Kushner, *Angels in America* (1992)
- Martin Macdonagh, *Beauty Queen of Leenane* (1996)

While these three plays, again, cannot be boxed as 'absurd', they have clearly defined qualities and links to the techniques pioneered by Beckett in *Endgame*, detailed as aspects of Miller's play above.

Hamm: Well?

Clov: Zero.

Hamm: It'd need to rain.

Clov: It won't rain.

[*Pause.*]

Hamm: Apart from that, how do you feel?

Clov: I don't complain.

Hamm: You feel normal?

Clov: [*Irritably.*] I tell you I don't complain!

Hamm: I feel a little queer. [*Pause.*] *Clov!*

Clov: Yes.

Hamm: Have you not had enough?

Clov: Yes! [*Pause.*] *Of what?*

Hamm: Of this…this…thing?

Clov: I always had. [*Pause.*] Not you?

Hamm: [*Gloomily.*] Then there's no reason for it to change.

Clov: It may end. [*Pause.*] All life long the same questions, the same answers.

Hamm: Get me ready. [*Clov does not move.*] Go and get the sheet. [*Clov does not move.*] Clov!

Clov: Yes.

Hamm: I'll give you nothing more to eat.

Clov: Then we'll die.

Hamm: I'll give you just enough to keep you from dying. You'll be hungry all the time.

Clov: Then we shan't die. [*Pause.*] I'll go and get the sheet. [*He goes towards the door.*]

Questions

AO1: Developing an informed response to the text

- What is happening in this scene?
- How do you react to the characters portrayed?

AO2: Understanding how structure, form and language shape meaning

- How do the stage directions contribute to the dramatic effect of the scene?
- What do you notice about the ways the dialogue is structured?
- The English title is taken from the last part of a chess game, when there are very few pieces left. What do you think could be the significance of this metaphor within this extract?
- This is a one-act play. From your reading of the extract, why do you think Beckett chose this dramatic structure for the play?

AO3: Exploring connections, comparisons and the interpretations of other readers

- Compare the presentation of Clov with that of other characters in suffering and/or of uncertain, lost or abandoned identity in other plays, novels and poems from your wider reading. You might like to start with the presentation of Billy Pilgrim in Kurt Vonnegut's *Slaughterhouse 5* in Chapter 5, Extract D.
- Compare the ways this scene presents the human condition with the ways it is presented in your wider reading on the struggle for identity.
- How far do you agree with the view that this play still offers a reflection on wider social issues because it considers not only feelings but human relationships and interactions?
- 'The Theatre of the Absurd does not show man in a historical, social, or cultural context; it does not communicate any general views of human life.' How far can you apply this view to the extract?

AO4: Understanding the significance and influence of contexts

- Explore the context of lost identities in domestic situations across the plays you have read for this option.
- How typical do you find this extract as an example of drama focused on issues of the 'self'?

The documentary approach – the drama of social realism revisited

A Raisin in the Sun, by Lorraine Hansberry (1959)

Lorraine Hansberry was an African American woman born in 1930, around the same time as the poet and autobiographer Maya Angelou. By the age of 29, Hansberry had written her first play, *A Raisin in the Sun*. In 1959, it was the first work by a black female writer to be premiered on Broadway, where it ran for nearly two years. What was unique about the play was its broad appeal. It introduced details of contemporary black American life to a largely white Broadway audience, and at the same time director Richards reported that it was the first play to attract a black audience.

By the age of 34, Hansberry had died from cancer. With *A Raisin in the Sun*, Lorraine Hansberry had made history. Her legacy ensures that she is not consigned to it.

Like O'Casey, Hansberry appears to tell the tale of a downtrodden family run by a matriarch in impossible circumstances. Both share a wider social setting of civil strife and poverty, and a dramatic setting of confined and inadequate housing. Hansberry's play was written at the dawn of the 1960s black civil rights movement, and is filled with hope and inspiration that the future would be different. Her tale presents a clearer conclusion of united 'resistance'. You can judge for yourself, by reading more contemporary literature (1980s onwards) from your wider reading list, whether African Americans (or indeed any marginalised group) are presented as achieving the social equality, unity and self-determination which had been Hansberry's political and dramatic ambitions.

The experiences in *A Raisin in the Sun* are also the subject of an actual lawsuit, *Hansberry* v. *Lee*, 311 U.S. 32 (1940), in which the Hansberry family fought for their right to stay in their chosen home amidst attempts to oust them in a legally sanctioned culture of segregated neighbourhoods in the Chicago of the mid 20th century.

The play itself deals with the working-class Younger family, as they dream of leaving behind the run-down tenement apartment where they have lived for many years. Their future neighbours in an all-white neighbourhood hire a character named Karl Lindner to liaise and to try to buy them out, to prevent the area from becoming integrated. Walter, the otherwise foolish and dreamy, underachieving son, is elected by the mother to deal with this situation. This is the point at which the extract starts.

Extract D

This edition was published by Methuen Drama in 2001.

From the ending of the play at the finale of Act 3, pages 111–12

> **Walter** …Well, Mr Lindner. (**Beneatha** *turns away.*) We called you (*there is a profound, simple groping quality in his speech*) because, well, me and my family… (*He looks around and shifts from one foot to the other.*) Well – we are very plain people…
>
> **Lindner** Yes –

Fig. 6.4 *Still from a production of* A Raisin in the Sun *of Walter and his mother*

Walter I mean – I have worked as a chauffeur most of my life – and my wife here, she does domestic work in people's kitchens. So does my mother. I mean – we are plain people…

Lindner Yes, Mr. Younger –

Walter (*really like a small boy, looking down at his shoes and then up at the man*) And – uh – well, my father, well, he was a labourer most of his life.

Lindner (*absolutely confused*) Uh, yes –

Walter (*looking down at his toes once again*) My father almost beat a man to death once because this man called him a bad name or something, you know what I mean?

Lindner No, I'm afraid I don't.

Walter (*finally straightening up*) Well, what I mean is that we come from people who had a lot of pride. I mean – we are very proud people. And that's my sister over there and she's going to be a doctor – and we are very proud –

Lindner Well – I am sure that is very nice, but –

Walter (*starting to cry and facing the man eye to eye*) What I am telling you is that we called you over here to tell you that we are very proud and that this is – this is my son, who makes the sixth generation of our family in this country, and that we have all thought about your offer and we have decided to move into our house because my father – my father – he earned it. (**Mama** *has her eyes closed and is rocking back and forth as though she were in church, with her head nodding the amen yes.*) We don't want to make no trouble for nobody or fight no causes – but we will try to be good neighbours. That's all we got to say. (*He looks the man absolutely in the eyes.*) We don't want your money. (*He turns and walks away from the man.*)

Further reading

On experience of social displacement in a range of domestic settings:

■ Jim Cartwright, *Road* (1986)

■ Brian Friel, *Dancing at Lughnasa* (1990)

■ Charlotte Keatley, *My Mother Said I Never Should* (1988)

■ Mark Ravenhill, *Citizenship* (2006)

■ Wole Soyinka, *Death and the King's Horseman* (1975) (from your coursework text list)

■ International Connections (contributor Jackie Kay), *New Plays for Young People* (2003)

■ Robert. Nemiroff, *To Be Young, Gifted and Black: Lorraine Hansberry in Her Own Words*. (1970)

Questions

AO1: Developing an informed response to the text

■ What is happening in this scene?

■ How do you respond to the events and to the characters?

AO2: Understanding how structure, form and language shape meaning

■ Explore the ways the dialogue is structured

■ What dramatic effects are created by the interactions of the characters and by the language they use?

■ Examine the ways in which Hansberry creates sympathy in this extract.

■ What use is made of stage directions?

AO3: Exploring connections, comparisons and the interpretations of other readers

■ Compare the presentation in this extract of injustice and inequality with ones you have come across in your wider reading.

■ Compare this presentation of a young black man experiencing a struggle to assert his identity with those you have encountered in your wider reading.

■ Compare this extract as an example of social realist drama to any other examples which you have read.

■ Hansberry was asked in interview: 'This is not really a Negro play; why, this could be about anybody! It's a play about people! What is your reaction? What do you say?' She answered: 'Well, I hadn't noticed the contradiction because I'd always been under the impression that Negroes *are* people. But actually it's an excellent question, because invariably that has been the point of reference.' How do you respond to this view?

AO4: Understanding the significance and influence of contexts

■ Explore the ways in which the context of 'resistance' within a struggle for identity is used here, and link to other 'resistance' literature from your wider reading.

■ This play was not published in Britain until 2001. Why do you think this might be?

■ The title comes from the opening lines of 'Dream Deferred', a poem by Langston Hughes (1902–67): 'What happens to a dream deferred? / Does it dry up / like a raisin in the sun?' Throughout the play runs the idea of dreams which are hard to achieve, as each member of the family attempts to find his or her identity amidst a number of difficult situations. How typical do you find this idea of deferred dreams in your wider reading on struggles for identity in modern literature?

The recent merge – late 20th- and 21st-century approaches

Angels in America, by Tony Kushner (1992)

Tony Kushner (1956–) is a truly 21st-century man. He represents the recent 'merge' in that he has taken all he can from the 20th-century dramatists and the sub-genres we have considered, understood how the modern media works and, in *Angels in America*, created a work which is self-consciously 'end of century'.

Even the title of Part One, 'Millennium Approaches', suggests he is well aware of the text's position in social and political history. The play was written towards the end of the 20th century and considers issues of importance for society at this time – in this play: AIDS, gay identity, Jewish identity, male and female identity, political corruption.

The play embodies social realism. However, there is more. The dramatic device of Angels is not merely a divine or moral presence, which drama has traditionally employed since its creation as a genre. It is used to dramatise the characters' experience of hallucinations, dreams and desires in a magic realist way. We are also offered the mental and physical isolation of many of the characters in fantastic settings, using nonsensical dialogue in a psychologically created 'reality' of their own. Here we are encouraged to suspend disbelief and enter the absurd world of the drama and its characters, as seen in Extract E2.

In the first extract, the McCarthyist New York lawyer, Roy Cohn, based on the actual historical person, is receiving a diagnosis of AIDS from his doctor.

In the second extract, Harper, the valium-addicted and unfulfilled agoraphobic wife of Joe (a court clerk who admires Roy and is himself a closeted Mormon gay man), has temporarily left her ordinary reality and gone to Antarctica with Mr Lies, her imaginary friend who is a travel agent.

Extract E1

This edition was published by Nick Herne Books in 1992.

From near the beginning, Act One, Scene Nine (edited). Pages 29–31

> **Roy** and **Henry**, *his doctor, in Henry's office.*
>
> **Henry** What are you doing, Roy?
>
> **Roy** No, say it. I mean it. Say: 'Roy Cohn, you are a homosexual.'
>
> > *Pause.*
> >
> > And I will proceed, systematically, to destroy your reputation and your practice and your career in New York State, Henry. Which you know I can do.
> >
> > *Pause.*
> >
> > …
>
> **Henry** Roy Cohn, you are…
> > You have had sex with men, many many times, Roy, and one of them, or any number of them, has made you very sick. You have AIDS.

Roy AIDS.

Your problem, Henry, is that you are hung up on words, on labels, that you believe they mean what they seem to mean. AIDS. Homosexual. Gay. Lesbian. You think these are names that tell you who someone sleeps with, but they don't tell you that.

Henry No?

Roy No. Like all labels they tell you one thing and one thing only: where does an individual so identified fit in the food chain, in the pecking order? Not ideology, or sexual taste, but something much simpler: clout. Not who I fuck or who fucks me, but who will pick up the phone when I call, who owes me favours. This is what a label refers to. Now to someone who does not understand this, the homosexual is what I am because I have sex with men. But really this is wrong. Homosexuals are not men who sleep with other men. Homosexuals are men who in fifteen years of trying cannot get a pissante anti-discrimination bill through City Council. Homosexuals are men who know nobody and who nobody knows. Who have zero clout. Does that sound like me, Henry?

Henry No.

Extract E2

From near the end, Act Three, Scene Four, pages 77–9

> **Harper** *in a very white, cold place, with a brilliant blue sky above; a delicate snowfall. She is dressed, for warmth, in layers upon layers of mismatched clothing. The sound of the sea, faint.*

…

Harper I want to stay here forever. Set up camp. Build things. Build a city, an enormous city made up of frontier forts, dark wood and green roofs and high gates made of pointed logs and bonfires burning on every street corner. I should build by a river. Where are the forests?

Mr Lies No timber here. Too cold. Ice, no trees.

Harper Oh details! I'm sick of details! I'll plant them and grow them. I'll live off caribou fat. I'll melt it over the bonfires and drink it from long, curved goat-horn cups. It'll be great. I want to make a new world here. So that I never have to go home again.

Mr Lies As long as it lasts. Ice has a way of melting…

Fig. 6.5 *Still from a production of* Angels in America

Harper No. Forever. I can have anything I want here – maybe even companionship, someone who has…desire for me. You, maybe.

Mr Lies It's against the by-laws of the International Order of the Travel Agents to get involved with clients. Rules are rules. Anyway, I'm not the one you really want.

Harper There isn't anyone…maybe an Eskimo. Who could ice-fish for food. And help me build a nest for when the baby comes.

Mr Lies There are no Eskimos in Antarctica. And you're not really pregnant. You made that up.

Harper Well all of this is made up. So if the snow feels cold I'm pregnant. Right? Here, I can be pregnant. And I can have any kind of a baby I want.

Mr Lies This is a retreat, a vacuum, its virtue is that it lacks everything; deep-freeze for feelings. You can be numb and safe here, that's what you came for. Respect the delicate ecology of your illusions.

Harper You mean like no Eskimo in Antarctica.

Mr Lies Correcto. Ice and snow, no Eskimo. Even hallucinations have laws.

Harper Well then who's that?

*The **Eskimo** appears.*

Mr Lies An Eskimo.

■ Questions

AO1: Developing an informed response to the text

■ What happens in the two scenes?

■ What are your thoughts and feelings about the characters presented?

AO2: Understanding how structure, form and language shape meaning

■ What is interesting about the ways the writer presents the characters?

■ What dramatic effects does he create from their interactions?

■ Explore the ways the dialogue is structured.

■ What use is made of stage directions?

■ What dramatic use is made of Henry and Mr Lies?

AO3: Exploring connections, comparisons and the interpretations of other readers

■ Contrast the use of dramatic technique and sub-genre in each extract.

■ Compare this extract to other portrayals of social disintegration and fractured identities in your wider reading.

■ 'Minorities issues for minority audiences.' How far do you think this criticism applies to the play, from reading the extracts?

■ How do you respond to the view that as Kushner simply borrows the styles of the past, he has created nothing new and gives us only 'smoke and mirrors'?

AO4: Understanding the significance and influence of contexts

■ What use does Kushner make of the context of struggles for identity?

■ What picture of end-of-20th-century life do we see here?

■ The subtitle of the play is 'A Gay Fantasia on National Themes'. How do we see these contexts in the extract you have read?

■ In what ways would you say this drama is typical of post-1980s drama that you have read on the struggle for identity in modern literature?

💡 *Summary*

In this chapter you have studied extracts from five different plays written about struggles for identity in modern literature. By now, you should have plenty of ideas about the style and subject matter of modern drama about the struggle for identity. You will be able to use these ideas in the context question in the AS exam. That question is the subject of the next chapter.

Further reading

Caryl Churchill, *Top Girls* (1982) (from your coursework text list)

Sarah Kane, *Complete Plays* (1998–2006)

Mark Ravenhill, *Shopping & F***ing* (1996)

7 Tackling the context question

The exam question

The **context question** in Unit 1 is at the heart of the AS English Literature course. It is the question where you have the opportunity to demonstrate and use the knowledge you have gained from all the reading you have done throughout the course.

The non-fiction text

All the reading and the exercises you have done in your course are relevant to the **context question**, which will be based on an extract from a **non-fiction** text. This might be any of the following:

- a diary
- a letter
- an autobiography
- a biography
- literary criticism
- a history text
- cultural commentary
- political travelogue
- scripted public speech (for example, Martin Luther King Jr, *I Have a Dream: Writings and Speeches That Changed the World*, on your wider reading list)
- transcript of a published interview (for example, Malcolm X, *Malcolm X Talks to Young People*, on your wider reading list).

The exam question

The question will include the extract, which you will need to read and study carefully. The examiner will give you information about how and when the extract came to be written. The question will then ask you to:

- consider the writer's **thoughts and feelings** about the struggle for identity and the ways in which she or he expresses them
- **compare** the extract to your wider reading, saying **how typical** you think it is of writing about the struggle for identity in modern literature. You should consider both **subject matter** and **style**.

The Assessment Objectives and the link to keywords in the exam question

You can see how all four Assessment Objectives are assessed in this question.

AO1: Communicating your informed, coherent response to the text is always tested in all questions.

AO2: Understanding and analysing how writers' choices of form, structure and language shape meaning is tested in the first bullet point, with the words **the ways she or he expresses them**, and in the second bullet point in the word **style**.

AO3: Exploring connections and comparisons as well as the interpretations of other readers is tested in the first bullet point, where you are asked to **consider** what the writer's thoughts and feelings might be, and in the second bullet point, where the examiner asks you to **compare** the extract to your wider reading.

AO4: Using your understanding of the significance and influence of contexts is tested in the second bullet point, where the examiner asks **how typical** this extract is of writing about the struggle for identity in modern literature.

Practising the skills

We are now going to look at **five** extracts so that you can see how to:

- read the extract carefully
- look for evidence of the writer's thoughts and feelings (**AO1**)
- analyse the writer's choices of form, structure and language, and how they shape meaning (**AO2**)
- make connections between the extract and your wider reading (**AO3**)
- assess the typicality of attitude and style of the extract (**AO4**).

Extract A – a diary

Bobby Sands, elected Independent MP for counties Fermanagh and South Tyrone, was a member of the IRA and went to prison in 1977 for an unproven link to a gun found near the scene of an explosion. He was part of the 1980–81 hunger strike by Republican Irish prisoners in the H-blocks of Long Kesh prison outside Belfast.

The strike was called to force the British government of the time to remove the criminal prisoner status and grant political prisoner status to Irish Republicans, imprisoned as part of the war between Northern Ireland and Britain. This included the political prisoner's right to wear his or her own clothes instead of prison uniform. They did not achieve their goals and 10 men died. One of them was Bobby Sands. On 5 May 1981, aged 27, he died, after 66 days of refusing food and medical intervention.

In 1982, an anthology of his writings, *Skylark Sing Your Lonely Song*, was published. It comprises diary entries, memoirs, poetry and short stories. It was written during his sentence on sheets of toilet paper with ballpoint pen refills, and subsequently smuggled out over a period of time.

The following extract is part of his diary and is taken from where he is reflecting on his situation as a prisoner.

> A stretch of tarmac surrounded by barbed wire and steel is the only view from my cell window. I'm told it's an exercise yard. I wouldn't know. In my fourteen months in H-Block, I haven't been allowed to walk in the fresh air. I am on 'cellular confinement' today. That is the three days out of every fourteen when my only possessions, three blankets and a mattress, are removed, leaving a blanket and a chamber pot.

Fig. 7.1 *Aerial photo of Long Kesh prison, Belfast*

I'm left to pass the day like this, from 7.30 a.m. to 8.30 p.m. How I spend my day is determined by the weather. If it's reasonably warm, it's possible to sit on the floor, stare at the white walls, and pass a few hours day dreaming. But otherwise I must spend my day continuously pacing the cell to prevent the cold chilling through to my bones. Even after my bedding is returned at 8.30 p.m. hours will pass before the circulation returns to my feet and legs.

Methods of passing the time are few and far between, so I am left with many hours of contemplation: good times, bad times, how I got here, but, most importantly, why I am here. During moments of weakness I try to convince myself that a prison uniform and conforming wouldn't be that bad. But the will to resist burns too strong within.

To accept the status of criminal would be to degrade myself and to admit that the cause that I believe in and cherish is wrong. When thinking of the men and women who sacrificed life itself, my suffering seems insignificant. There have been many attempts to break my will but each one has made me even more determined. I know my place is here with my comrades.

■ Further reading

Diaries and memoirs:

- ■ *Women's Stories from the North of Ireland,* edited by Silvia Calamati (as a result of interviews) (2002)

- ■ Anne Frank, *The Diary of a Young Girl* (translated from the Dutch) (1947)

- ■ Nawal al-Saadawi, *Memoirs from the Women's Prison* (translated from the Arabic) (1984)

- ■ Alice Walker, *The Same River Twice: Honoring the Difficult* (1996)

■ Questions

- ■ What thoughts and feelings does Sands express about his identity as a prisoner? (AO1)
- ■ What do you notice about the ways he expresses his ideas? (AO2)
- ■ What kind of vocabulary does he use? (AO2)
- ■ What influence do you think the setting might have on his viewpoint? (AO4)
- ■ What connections can you make between the fight for political liberation and personal freedom he expresses here and views expressed in your wider reading? (AO3)
- ■ Which texts support his view? Try to think of at least **one** prose, **one** drama and **one** poetry text/extract. (AOs 3 and 4)
- ■ Which texts challenge the key point about resistance which he makes here? Try to think of at least **one** prose, **one** drama and **one** poetry text/extract. (AOs 3 and 4)
- ■ Assess the **typicality** of the extract as a diary and as part of the literature of a struggle for identity. (AO4)
- ■ If you are working in a group, share and compare your findings.

Extract B – a biography

Radclyffe Hall's publishers and novel, *The Well of Loneliness*, a story of lesbian life and love set in her own society, were put on trial and banned under Parliament's 'Obscene Publications Act' in 1928, an act of literary censorship. The author of Hall's biography, Diana Souhami, claims that far from being a racy read, 'the sexiest line in it [Hall's novel] is "and that night they were not divided"'. Souhami takes the modern view that it was not the book or even a notion of sexual obscenity that was on trial, but the lifestyle and sexuality of its author.

This extract covers an episode in Radclyffe Hall's life which occurred in 1920, when she was 36. St John Lane Fox-Pitt and Sir Ernest Troubridge, whose wife had left him for Hall, had publicly declared her a 'grossly immoral woman'. It is from here in the biography that the extract has been taken.

Radclyffe Hall was summoned and told of Fox-Pitt's words. They were catalytic. Here, demeaned, was her life. She acted with a forcefulness thought to be the prerogative of admirals and lords. She demanded that he withdraw his accusations. He refused. Like others after him, he underestimated her. She said her honour and Mabel Batten's were impugned and she gave the eighteenth-century equivalent of a challenge to a duel. She saw her solicitor, Sir George Lewis, and took out a slander action.

Fox-Pitt and Troubridge went into a tizz. Money gave Radclyffe Hall power to use the law and they knew it. She challenged them to make their accusations public and to justify their prejudice. She had no fear of the court's judgement or publicity from such a case. Had the price been crucifixion or public pillory she would have paid it. She was not going to be embarrassed into silence. She was a homophobe's nightmare: dykish, rich, unyielding, outspoken, successful with women and caring not at all for the small vanities of men. Mabel Batten* would have been placatory, smoothed feathers and soothed tempers. Radclyffe Hall wanted justice, honour and scruple to resound.

Fig. 7.2 *Radclyffe Hall*

* a lover of Radclyffe Hall's

Questions

- What key point does Souhami make about the struggle for Radclyffe Hall's identity? (AO1)
- What do you notice about the ways Souhami expresses her knowledge and opinions? (AO2)
- What kind of vocabulary does she use? (AO2)
- What connections can you make between ideas about forbidden love as Souhami expresses them here and views expressed in your wider reading? You might like to start with those texts that address the notions of 'perversity' and 'immorality'. (AO3)
- Using Extract A in Chapter 5 from *Oranges Are Not the Only Fruit* (1984), Extract E in Chapter 4, the poem 'Funeral Blues' (1936) and Extract E1 in Chapter 6, the drama *Angels in America* (1992), compare and contrast (AO3) the presentation (AO2) of lesbian and gay identity (AO1 and AO4) in these four extracts.
- Assess the **typicality** of the extract in the literature of a struggle for identity. (AO4)
- What influence do you think the time of writing this biography might have on Souhami's viewpoint? (AO4)
- If you are working in a group, share and compare your findings.

Further reading

Source material:
- Radclyffe Halll, *The Well of Loneliness* (1928)

Unbanned literature in the same year about lesbian sexuality:
- Virginia Woolf, *Orlando* (1928)

A contrast in era, culture and subsequent depiction of gay and lesbian life:

Novels
- James Baldwin, *Go Tell it on the Mountain* (1954)
- Alan Hollinhurst, *The Swimming Pool Library* (1988)
- Patrick McCabe, *Breakfast on Pluto* (1998)
- Alice Walker, *The Color Purple* (1983)
- Jeanette Winterson, *Oranges Are Not the Only Fruit* (1984)

Drama
- Claire Dowie, *Why is John Lennon Wearing a Skirt?* (1996)
- Mark Ravenhill, *Citizenship* (post-1990)

Extract C – a political travelogue

The political travelogue differs from other travelogues in that the writer attempts to grasp and present to the reader the political situation and its effect on the people in the region travelled. The focus is a commentary on current affairs rather than simply a guidebook to the area for holiday or leisure travel.

Adhaf Soueif is an Egyptian journalist and commentator living in London. This extract is taken from *Mezzaterra,* an anthology of her essays between 1981 and 2004, and is entitled 'Under the Gun: A Palestinian Journey.' Soueif has travelled to Palestine and is trying to gain access to the old part of the city of Al-Khalil (or Hebron), which is road-blocked and besieged by the Israeli army, to write an article for the *Guardian* newspaper.

The photographers tell me that when there is going to be any real action the soldiers simply shoo away the observers. A mobile rings and it is my guide begging me to come back.

I want to go into the old city but my guide and driver are fearful and reluctant. As we argue in the street a woman stops and asks where I'm from. I'm an Egyptian from London writing a piece for a British paper. 'Then you should take her in,' she says, and starts to describe a route.

They will not listen to her. An imposing man in a grey cashmere overcoat appears. They seem awed by him. I later learn that he is a Palestinian journalist who's been shot in five separate incidents.* The woman tells him what's happening and he says, 'Come on, chaps. It's your duty to take her in. You've got Israeli licence plates. She's got a British passport. Take her in.'

Reluctantly they make a detour and try to drive into the old city. Forty thousand people live here under curfew. Twelve thousand children cannot go to school. Fifteen mosques are closed. In the centre, armed, live what Israel says are 400 settlers** and the Palestinians say are 100. All this is for their benefit.

'If the army were to go away', I ask, 'and the settlers were content to live here among you, would you let them?'

Fig. 7.3 *A Palestinian protestor*

'They wouldn't. They would go away.'

'But if they wanted to stay, could they?'

'They've taken people's homes. If you could go into the centre you would see families camped by their homes, refusing to leave, and the settlers throw rubbish on them and beat them up. They're not even proper settlers; they are religious students, mostly from the United States, volunteering to come for one or two years to do their religious duty by being here—'

*This was Mazin Da'na who worked for Reuters. He was killed by the Americans in 2003 while filming in Baghad.
**The settlers here are Israeli citizens who live in Palestinian settlements, or visitors/guests of Israel who temporarily moved into Palestinian areas.

Questions

- What thoughts and feelings does Soueif express about the struggle for identity in Palestine? (AO1)
- What do you notice about the ways she expresses what she sees and discovers? (AO2)
- What kind of vocabulary does she use? (AO2)
- What influence do you think the setting might have on her viewpoint? (AO4)
- What connections can you make between ideas about people under fire as she expresses it here and views expressed in your wider reading? You might like to start with those texts that address the notions of 'terrorist', 'victim' and 'bystander'. (AO3)
- Using Extract D from Chapter 4, 'The School Among the Ruins', written in 2001, compare (AO3) the presentation (AO2) of subject matter and ideas (AO1 and AO4).
- Which texts challenge the ideas about 'suffering' and 'resistance' which Soueif makes here? Try to think of at least **one** prose, **one** drama and **one** poetry text/extract. (AOs 3 and 4)
- Assess the **typicality** of the extract as part of the literature of a struggle for identity. (AO4)
- If you are working in a group, share and compare your findings.

Further reading

Travelogues or eyewitness accounts of history texts on current affairs:

- David Beresford, *Ten Men Dead: The Story of the 1981 Hunger Strike* (also a journalist) (1987)
- Che Guevara, *The Motorcycle Diaries* (translated from Spanish) (1952)
- Salman Rushdie, *The Jaguar Smile: A Nicaraguan Journey* (1987)

Extract D – a cultural commentary

This extract comes from *The Female Eunuch* by the writer, broadcaster and academic Germaine Greer. It was originally published in 1970, but has since been reprinted several times. This edition is from 2006 and includes the author's 'Foreword to the 21st Anniversary Edition', which was originally printed in the 1991 edition.

The Foreword is Greer's updated commentary on the subject of the text – the social position of women – as she sees it 20 years after she first wrote the book. This extract comes from that Foreword.

> The freedom I pleaded for twenty years ago was freedom to be a person, with the dignity, integrity, nobility, passion, pride that constitute personhood. Freedom to run, shout, to talk loudly and sit with your knees apart. Freedom to know and love the earth and all that swims, lies and crawls upon it. Freedom to learn and freedom to teach. Freedom from fear, freedom from hunger, freedom of speech and freedom of belief. Most of the women in the world are still afraid, still hungry, still mute and loaded by religion with all kinds of fetters, masked, muzzled, mutilated and beaten. The Female Eunuch does not deal with poor women (for when I wrote it I did not know them) but with the women of the rich world, whose oppression is seen by poor women as freedom.
>
> The sudden death of communism in 1989–90 catapulted poor women in the world over into consumer society, where there is no protection for mothers, for the aged, for the disabled, no commitment to health care or education or raising the standards of living for the whole population. In those two years millions of women saw the bottom fall out of their world; though they lost their child support, their pensions, their hospital benefits, their day care, their protected jobs, and the very schools and hospitals where they worked closed down, there was

Fig. 7.4 *Germaine Greer*

no outcry. They had freedom to speak but no voice. They had freedom to buy essential services with money they did not have, freedom to indulge in the oldest form of private enterprise, prostitution, prostitution of body, mind and soul to consumerism, or else freedom to starve, freedom to beg.

■ Questions

■ What key point does Greer make about the struggle for female identity? (AO1)

■ What do you notice about the structure and the ways she expresses her ideas? (AO2)

■ What kind of vocabulary does she use? (AO2)

■ What influence do you think the time of writing might have on her viewpoint? (AO4)

■ What connections can you make between ideas about the social position of women as she expresses it here and views expressed in your wider reading? You might like to start with those texts that address the notions of 'powerful' and 'powerless'. (AO3)

■ Which texts support Greer's view that not all social groups have equal status?

■ The writer and political thinker Angela Carter described Greer as a 'clever fool'. Can you think of any texts which support this view (of saying stupid things in a knowledgeable way)? Try to think of at least **one** prose, **one** drama and **one** poetry text/extract. (AOs 3 and 4)

■ Assess the **typicality** of the extract as an example of literature about the struggle for identity. (AO4)

■ If you are working in a group, share and compare your findings.

■ Further reading

Cultural commentary:

■ Beverly Bryan, Suzanne Scafe and Stella Dadzie, *The Heart of the Race* (1985)

■ Edward W. Said, *Culture and Imperialism* (1993)

■ Amrit Wilson, *Dreams, Questions, Struggles. South Asian Women in Britain* (2006)

Extract E – an autobiography

This extract is taken from *I Know Why the Caged Bird Sings*, the first volume of autobiography from the African American writer Maya Angelou. It was first published by Virago in 1969, but recalls Angelou's childhood during the 1930s–1940s, beginning with her depiction of life in the segregated southern state of Arizona.

Fig. 7.5 *African American children at school in the 1930s*

When I was three and Bailey four, we had arrived in the musty little town, wearing tags on our wrists which instructed—'To Whom It May Concern'—that we were Marguerite and Bailey Johnson Jr., from Long Beach, California, en route to Stamps, Arkansas, c/o Mrs. Annie Henderson.

Our parents had decided to put an end to their calamitous marriage, and Father shipped us home to his mother. A porter had been charged with our welfare—he got off the train the next day in Arizona—and our tickets were pinned to my brother's inside coat pocket.

I don't remember much of the trip, but after we reached the segregated southern part of the journey, things must have looked up. Negro passengers, who always travelled with loaded lunch boxes felt sorry for 'the poor little motherless darlings' and plied us with cold fried chicken and potato salad.

> Years later I discovered that the United States had been crossed thousands of times by frightened Black children travelling alone to their newly affluent parents in Northern cities, or back to grandmothers in Southern towns when the urban North reneged on its economic promises.

Questions

- What key features does Angelou describe in this extract about the struggle for identity of African Americans ? (AO1)
- What do you notice about the structure and ways she expresses her thoughts and feelings in the extract? (AO2)
- What kind of vocabulary does she use? (AO2)
- What influence do you think the time of writing might have on her viewpoint? (AO4)
- What connections can you make between ideas about racial identity as she expresses it here and views expressed in your wider reading? You might like to start with those texts that address the notions of 'segregation' and 'displacement'. (AO3)
- Which texts compare with this extract? Try to think of at least **one** prose, **one** drama and **one** poetry text/extract. (AOs 3 and 4)
- Which texts contrast with this extract? Try to think of at least **one** prose, **one** drama and **one** poetry text/extract. (AOs 3 and 4)
- Assess the typicality (AO4) of the extract for subject matter (AO1) and sub-genre (AO2).
- If you are working in a group, share and compare your findings.

Further reading

Autobiography

- Zora Neale Hurston, *Dust Tracts on a Road* (1942)

Summary

The extracts

- In this chapter we have looked closely at five extracts: diary, biography, political travelogue, cultural commentary and autobiography. The questions and activities have been devised to encourage you to look at the extracts closely and in ways that will help you in the exam.

Variety of response

- If you have shared your thoughts with other students, you will no doubt have discovered perspectives other than your own, and you will have realised that there are many different ways in which wider reading can be used. Examiners expect to come across many different ways of approaching the question and to read a variety of answers. There is no 'right' answer; but they expect you to write relevantly, addressing the keywords, and to select appropriate supporting material.

The question

- Remember that in the actual exam the question will contain two simple bullet points. In order to answer the question, however, you will need to go through all the processes that have followed each of the extracts in this chapter.

Chapter 8 contains an example of the context question as it will appear in the exam under 'Section A: Contextual Linking'.

Conclusion: a specimen paper

- Reviews the skills and knowledge gained through your AS English Literature course and studying this book.

- Introduces a specimen exam paper where you can practise your skills and identify where you might need to improve them.

- Looks at ways of approaching the exam paper.

- Explains how you will be assessed.

Link

In Chapter 2 we explored the kinds of questions that will be asked on your set poetry text; one of the suggested activities was to make up your own questions that address the three relevant Assessment Objectives.

In Chapter 7 we looked in detail at the kinds of extracts you could expect to find in the context question on the exam paper.

Introduction

By the time you have worked through this book and are approaching your AS English Literature exam, you will need to start thinking about how you are going to:

- use the knowledge you have gathered, through your study of the set texts and your wider reading of literature on 'the struggle for identity', in the exam

- demonstrate the skills you have been practising through the activities.

Your coursework essays should now be written, but remember that your knowledge of your two chosen coursework texts – the play and the novel – is relevant to the context question on the exam paper. In addition, you should have a Reading Log of all the wider reading you have done in prose, poetry and drama on the struggle for identity; this log will either be in the form of written notes or a file on the computer. These notes should form the basis of your revision for the exam paper.

The specimen paper

The best way to prepare for the real exam is to practise answering questions of the type that you will be asked. You can, of course, make up your own questions – alone, or in a group, and with the help of your teacher. If you do this, you need to follow the models provided in this book.

What follows now is a complete specimen paper. How you use it will be for you to decide. You and your teacher may wish to use it as a 'mock' exam, sitting down and writing for two hours under exam conditions. Or you may wish to look at the questions alone or in a group, brainstorming what materials you might use, how you might structure your answers, and then comparing notes, before you write the relevant essays.

Here is the paper. Read through it carefully and closely.

AQA Examination-style questions

Unit 1 Texts in Context

Time allowed 2 hours

Candidates must answer **two** questions:

■ the compulsory question in **Section A**

■ one question in **Section B**.

Option C: The Struggle for Identity in Modern Literature

Section A: Contextual Linking

Answer Question 1.

1   Read the following extract carefully. It is taken from *The Words of Martin Luther King, Jr.* (speeches, sermons and articles written by Martin Luther King, Jr, a black American civil rights leader). In this speech, Dr King is publicly addressing 250,000 people after a march on the capital Washington about equal rights for black people in America.

In your answer you should:

■ consider the writer's thoughts and feelings about the struggle for identity and the ways in which he expresses them compare this extract to your wider reading, saying how typical you think it is of the literature of World War One. You should consider both subject matter and style.

(45 marks)

'I have a dream'
August 28th, 1963, Washington D.C.

...I say to you today, my friends, so even though we face the difficulties of today and tomorrow, I still have a dream. It is a dream deeply rooted in the American dream. I have a dream that one day this nation will rise up and live out the true meaning of its creed: 'We hold these truths to be self evident; that all men are created equal.' I have a dream that one day, on the red hills of Georgia, sons of former slaves and the sons of former slave owners will be able to sit together at the table of brotherhood. I have a dream that one day even the state of Mississippi, a state sweltering with the heat of injustice, sweltering with the heat of oppression, will be transformed into an oasis of freedom and justice. I have a dream that my four little children will one day live in a nation where they will not be judged by the colour of their skin but by the content of their character.

I have a dream today.

...And when this happens, and when we allow freedom to ring, when we let it ring from every village and every hamlet, from every state and every city, we will be able to speed up that day when all of God's children, black men and white men, Jews and Gentiles, Protestants and Catholics, will be able to join hands and sing in the words of that old Negro spiritual, 'Free at last! Free at last! Thank God Almighty, we are free at last!'

Option C: The Struggle for Identity in Modern Literature
Section B: Poetry

And Still I Rise – Maya Angelou

Answer one question from this section.

2   How far do you agree that 'Still I Rise' is the key to the whole collection?

You should consider both subject matter and style.

(45 marks)

Or

3   The black American writer James Baldwin assessed Angelou's style and subject matter as 'Black, bitter and beautiful, she speaks of our survival'.

How far do you agree that this view applies to *And Still I Rise*?

(45 marks)

Or

The World's Wife – Carol Ann Duffy

4   Duffy published 'Mrs Midas' (page 11) several years before its inclusion in *The World's Wife*.

To what extent do you agree with the view that, in terms of subject matter and style, this poem is the key to the whole collection?

(45 marks)

Or

5   How far do you agree with the view that *The World's Wife* is 'nothing but feminist propaganda'?

In your answer, you should **either** refer to **two** or **three** poems in detail **or** range more widely across the whole collection.

(45 marks)

Or

Skirrid Hill – Owen Sheers

6   How far do you agree with the view that 'Mametz Wood' (page 1) is the key to this collection?

You should consider both subject matter and style.

(45 marks)

Or

7   To what extent do you agree that in these poems Sheers explores lost identity?

You may use 'The Singing Men' (page 50) as a starting point if you wish.

(45 marks)

END OF QUESTIONS

Approaching the paper

Before you start to think about the two questions you will answer, you need to consider your approach to the exam paper. This vital preparation should include:

■ familiarity with the **Assessment Objectives** and the **marking grid**

■ revision of all the texts you have read during the course – this will include your two coursework texts

■ experimenting with and trying out different ways of brainstorming and planning your essays

■ thinking about the use of time in the exam – a good guide is to divide the time equally between the questions, and to spend roughly 15 minutes planning and organising each answer and 45 minutes writing it

■ being aware that you are the **maker of meaning** when answering these questions. The key aspect of the marking grid that you need to understand is that there is no **prescribed content**. All the questions invite you to select and organise the material that you wish to use in your answer. The examiner's task is to judge how well your choices of material and your analysis of your texts enable you to construct an argument in response to the specific question set. Obviously, your answer needs to be relevant and well written, so we are going to spend some time now looking at all the questions on the paper, finding the **focus** and identifying the **keywords**.

Link

The Assessment Objectives and marking grid are explained in Chapter 1.

Activity

First, try to identify the focus and keywords of each question. You may find it useful to do the following activities. Then you can check what you have identified with the suggested answers below.

1 Keywords

Study each of the seven questions and either write down, highlight or underline what you consider to be the **keywords** of the questions. The **keywords** need to inform all your planning (and then your writing), since they are the way the **Assessment Objectives** are signalled in the question.

2 The focus

Then move on to identify the **focus** of the question.

In Question 1 this will be the extract and its links to your wider reading.

In the poetry question, the **focus** of your essay will be:

■ either a **critical opinion** about a **named poem** and its relation to other poems in the collection

■ or a **critical opinion** about the collection in general.

You could do this work alone, or by working in a group and sharing your ideas.

When you have finished you should move on and check how far your ideas match the ones suggested below.

■ Keywords, focus and strategies in the examination room

We will now go through the questions in turn and look at the focus and the keywords of each question. Then we will look at strategies for answering the question.

Section A

Question 1 (the compulsory question)

The **focus** of this question is an extract from a public speech by Martin Luther King, Jr in 1963, printed in *The Words of Martin Luther King, Jr.*, as well as the **connections** you can make to your wider reading.

The **keywords** in the question are:

- writer's thoughts and feelings
- ways he expresses them
- compare to your wider reading
- how typical
- subject matter and style.

Your strategy in the examination room should be, above all, to read closely and to plan and organise effectively. Your success in the exam will depend on this. Here is our advice:

1 Take enough time to read the question very carefully, underlining or highlighting the keywords.

2 Then read the extract very closely and consider what Martin Luther King, Jr is writing about (**the subject matter**), paying particular attention to his thoughts and feelings.

3 Then you should turn to a consideration of how he expresses those thoughts and feelings (**his style**).

4 When you have read the extract closely several times and have made detailed notes on it, you should start to consider what connections come to mind with your wider reading in the literature of 'The Struggle for Identity in Modern Literature'.

5 First think of similarities in your wider reading in the areas of:
- thoughts and feelings
- genre – a speech in this case
- writing style
- the gender of the writer
- time of writing.

6 Then turn to 'differences' in your wider reading, using the same categories.

7 These notes will help you to decide how typical the extract is of writing from or about 'The Struggle for Identity in Modern Literature', and will form the basis of your essay.

8 Remember that all four Assessment Objectives are tested in this question, so as you plan, and then as you write, you need to be sure that you:
- shape your ideas into a coherent, well-illustrated answer
- explore the ways King and other writers use form, structure and language to shape meaning

■ **Link**

Turn back to Chapter 1 and look at the advice about close reading. Use those questions to support your close reading in this section.

■ make connections between the King extract and your wider reading

■ trace the influence of the context of the struggle for identity on King's extract.

Section B

All the poetry questions target the same Assessment Objectives, and we will return to these after we have considered the focus and the keywords of each question.

And Still I Rise: Maya Angelou

Question 2

The **focus** of this question is the poem 'Still I Rise' and the rest of the collection.

The **keywords** are:

■ how far do you agree

■ key to the whole collection

■ subject matter and style.

Question 3

The **focus** of this question is a wide selection of poems.

The **keywords** of the question are:

■ black, bitter and beautiful

■ she speaks of our survival

■ how far do you agree.

The World's Wife: Carol Ann Duffy

Question 4

The **focus** of this question is the poem 'Mrs Midas' and the rest of the collection.

The **keywords** are:

■ to what extent do you agree

■ key to the whole collection

■ subject matter and style.

Question 5

The **focus** of this question is either two or three poems or a wide range of poems.

The **keywords** are:

■ how far do you agree

■ nothing but feminist propaganda

Skirrid Hill: Owen Sheers

Question 6

The **focus** of this question is the poem 'Mametz Wood' and the rest of the selection.

The **keywords** are:

■ how far do you agree

■ key to this collection.

Question 7

The **focus** of this question is a wide selection and, if you wish, 'The Singing Men'.

The **keywords** are:

■ to what extent do you agree

■ lost identity.

In Section B, you have to answer **one** of these six questions. All these questions test the same three Assessment Objectives, so whichever question you answer, you should adopt the following strategy.

1 Read the question carefully, underlining or highlighting the **keywords**.

2 Look carefully at the **critical opinion** in the question and choose the poems that will help you to construct the argument of your answer.

3 Remember that the question will ask you **how far or to what extent do you agree**, so you will need to consider both sides of the argument and find material to support these views.

4 Three Assessment Objectives are assessed in this answer, so you need to ensure that:

■ you construct a well-argued, well-informed, coherent essay

■ you explore the ways the poet's choices of form, structure and language shape meaning

■ you compare and connect the poems in your text and explore interpretations of them.

■ Assessment

You may want to ask your teacher to assess your answers to the specimen questions, you may wish to assess your own work or to work in a group with your peers, looking at each other's work.

Here is a summary of the bands of achievement:

■ If your work has the features of Band 1 work – **inaccurate, irrelevant, assertive** – you will not be writing at the required standard for AS.

■ If your work is **narrative, descriptive and generalised** in its approach to the text, it will be assessed in Band 2 of the grid.

■ If you are starting to **explore and analyse** the texts and to present your argument in a **coherent** fashion, your work will be assessed in Band 3.

■ If your work is **coherent, cogent, mature, fluent and sophisticated**, it will be assessed in Band 4.

You can go on from here to make up your own questions and practise selecting material, planning, organising and writing your responses. The purpose of this book, and of your whole AS English Literature course, has been to encourage you to develop as an **informed, independent reader**, and, if you have followed the advice and taken part in the activities, you can be confident that you will have achieved that, and that your success in the AS course is assured.

> ■ **Link**
>
> However you choose to assess your work, you need to go back to Chapter 1 and remind yourself of the skills profiles of the different bands of achievement.

Glossary

A

Active creator: a maker of meaning; a reader who has individual ideas rather than re-cycling the ideas of others.

Active engagement: thinking for yourself about the text you are reading.

Adaptation: a modified literary text in a different genre to the original work; usually a novel or a play made into a film.

Analyse: *see* 'close reading'.

Assertive: *see* 'unsupported assertion'.

Assessment objectives: these identify the skills which candidates need to display in their examination answers.

Autobiography: a non-fiction text which presents a first person version of the writer's life.

B

Background: *see* 'context'.

Ballad: a simple narrative poem written in the third person.

Biographical notes: a short summary of a writer's life.

Biography: a non-fiction text which presents a third person version of the subject's life.

Brainstorm: gather together a range of relevant ideas before organising them into a coherent response.

C

Characters: the people in a novel, invented by the writer – they are not real people.

Chronological: telling the story in the order that the events occurred.

Close reading: focused, analytical reading which discovers multiple meanings through exploration of textual detail.

Cogent: convincing and persuasive; powerfully argued.

Coherent: well-organised; clear and well argued.

Collective address: signified by the use of 'we' towards the audience.

Comedy: a play with a happy ending, its main purpose is to make the audience laugh.

Context question: an examination question which requires the candidate to respond to an unprepared non-fiction prose extract and to place it in a wider literary and historical context.

Context: the cultural, social and historical background to a literary text.

Creative transformational writing: an imaginative response to a literary text which shows your knowledge and understanding through the ways in which you re-creation reflects the original text.

Critical opinion: a quotation from a literary critic, to which you should give balanced consideration in your poetry answer.

Cultural commentary: a non-fiction text which presents the writer's observations on a contemporary cultural, literary or artistic issue.

D

Descriptive: an answer which gives an account of the text rather than analysing the writer's techniques.

Detective thriller: a sub-genre of fiction. These texts relate to detectives or their work and include a high degree of intrigue and suspense

Diary: a first person account of events, not usually intended for publication.

Direct address: addressing the reader as 'you'.

Documentary style: a factual account of events.

Drama: *see* 'genre'.

Dramatic monologue: a narrative poem written in the first person.

Dystopia: a society which is undesirable and has broken away from the social norms that many in our society would currently accept.

E

Essay: a short non-fiction text which treats its subject in a formal, systematic manner.

Explore: *see* 'close reading'.

F

First person narrator: an author who writes in role as one of the characters in the story, using the first person (e.g. I, we) to present a perspective on events.

Flashback: an interruption of the chronological sequence to interject events from the past.

Fluent: written with impressive confidence and clarity.

Focus: the specific aspect of a literary text which you will write about in your coursework.

Frame narrator: a first person narrator whose story includes a second narrative related by a different character.

Free verse: poetry which adopts any form, any metre, any rhythm.

G

Gender: sex – either male or female.

Generalised: an answer which is broadly accurate but fails to consider the detail of the text.

Genre: the type of a literary text. The three main literary genres are prose, poetry and drama. These genres can be sub-divided: for instance, prose can be classified as fiction or non-fiction – and, in turn, fiction can be split into sub-genres such as the Gothic novel and the Bildungsroman.

H

How typical: in what ways is the extract similar to, or different from, other writing of the same historical period?

I

Imaginative re-construction: *see* 'creative transformational writing'.

Inaccurate: an answer containing errors.

Independent: *see* 'active creator'.

Informed response: a response based on knowledge and understanding.

Inter-textuality: the establishment of links and connections between different literary texts.

Interview: a spoken word forms which, in transcript, constitutes a non-fiction text.

Introduction: an integral, informative opening section of a text.

Irrelevant: an answer that has nothing to do with the question that was asked.

K

Key words: the most important words in an examination question: the ones you must address in your answer.

L

Literary criticism: a non-fiction text which analyses literature in an academic manner.

Literature in translation: texts that were originally written in a language other than English.

M

Magic realist: a narrative style used in some novels and some plays which combine features that are easy to believe and represent reality (realism) and features that may seem impossible to believe and don't appear possible (magic). For example – believable characters experiencing recognisable feelings in an unbelievable setting, or fantasy characters experiencing magical events in a very ordinary setting.

Maker of meaning: *see* 'active creator'.

Marking grid: a tool which enables examiners to measure candidates' abilities according to the Assessment Objectives and then award the appropriate marks.

Mature: fully developed; displaying a mastery of the text.

Melodrama: an exaggerated form of drama based on simple characters, excessive emotions and over-acting.

Memoir: a first person account of events, usually intended for publication.

Multiple narrators: the author tells the story through several different first person narrators.

N

Named poem: some examination questions name a specific poem as the subject for debate. You will also need to link it to other poems in your answer.

Narrative: the story and the way it is told.

Non-chronological: mixing up the order of events to create narrative effects.

O

Omniscient/third person narrator: an author who knows everything the characters are thinking and uses the third person (e.g.: he, she, they) to reveal the characters' thoughts and feelings to the reader.

Open letter: a published letter which any member of the reading public can access.

P

Pastiche: a text which imitates the work of another writer.

Personal informed interpretation: a coursework response with a focus on what you find interesting about a particular aspect of the text.

Personal response: a response which features your own relevant ideas about a text.

Plot: the things that happen in a novel.

Poetry: *see* 'genre'.

Preface: a piece of writing at the beginning of a text which is not integral to the text itself.

Prescribed content: specific ideas, characters or quotations which are guaranteed to earn a candidate marks in the examination. (There is no prescribed content for this paper: the mark is determined by the overall quality of a candidate's response.)

Prose: *see* 'genre'.

Realism: the presentation of life as it really is, rather than in a romantic or glamorous way.

Romanticism: a revolutionary literary movement of the late eighteenth and early nineteenth centuries. Romantic writers are noted for their celebration of the individual imagination and their spiritual approach to nature.

S

Satire: a humorous play which mocks or questions contemporary values.

Science fiction: a sub-genre of fiction. These texts consider the impact of science (real or imaginary) on society or individuals.

Setting: the places in which the events of a novel occur.

Shared context: the background common to a collection of texts from the same historical period.

Simultaneous: occurring at the same time.

Skimpy: thin, superficial, underdeveloped.

Social drama: a play presenting the state of contemporary society (*see also* Social Realism).

Social realism: the presentation of society and everyday life as they really are.

Sophisticated: subtle and skilful; not afraid to tackle the complexities of the text; reading at a very high level.

Speech: a spoken word form which, in transcript, constitutes a non-fiction text.

Stream of consciousness: a modern literary technique which presents the reader with a character's uninterrupted thoughts.

Structure: the ways in which the distinctive features of a text, such as its narrative or its chronology, are organised.

Style: the writer's choices of language, form and structure – and the effects created by these choices.

Suspension of disbelief: a state in which the audience/reader is able to temporarily disregard their notions of what is unreal and impossible in order to accept fantasy and magic.

T

Thematically: grouped and arranged according to theme or subject matter.

Travelogue: a first person account of the writer's travels.

Trilogy: a sequence of three novels, often featuring the same characters.

Typicality: the ways in which a text is characteristic of the writing of a particular historical period.

U

Unsupported assertion: a claim that is not backed up by any evidence from the text.

Utopia: a perfect society.

V

Vernacular: the normal spoken language or dialect of a group, which may vary from the usual literary, cultured language.

W

Wide reading: reading a range of different texts, in all three literary genres, within the shared context. A list of suggested wide reading texts is contained in Chapter 1.